Table of Contents

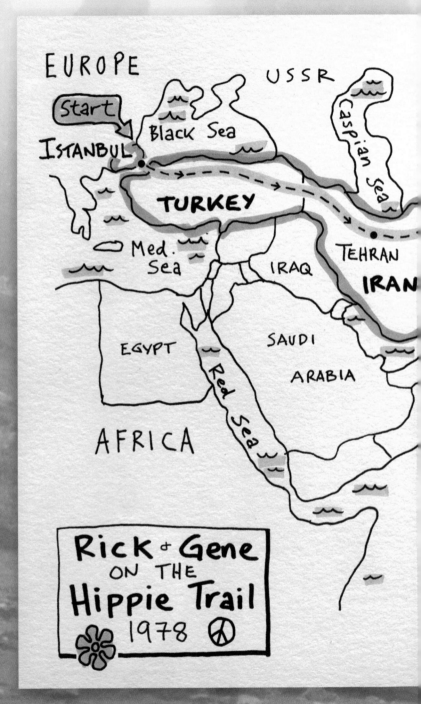

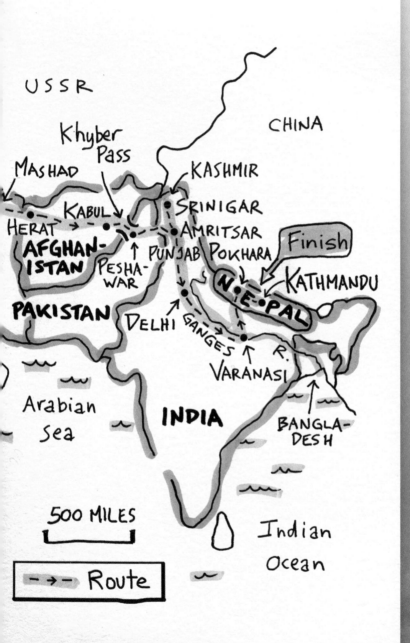

The Trip — July 13 to Sept 8, 1978

July 13 Travel to Frankfurt

14 Meet Gene in Frankfurt

15 Train: Germany — Belgrade

16 Belgrade — Plovdiv

17 Plovdiv, Bulgaria

18 Plovdiv

19 Istanbul

20 Istanbul

21 Bus through Turkey

22 Bus through Turkey

23 Bus Erzurum — Iran

24 Tehran, Iran

25 Tehran

26 Teheran

27 Bus Teheran — Mashad

28 Meshad

July 29 Meshad — Herat

30 Herat, Afganistan

31 Herat

August 1 Bus: Herat — Kabul

2 Kabul

3 Kabul

4 Kabul — Rawalpindi, Pakistan

5 Rawalpindi — Lahore

6 Lahore — Amritsar, INDIA!

7 Jammu — Srinagar, Kashmir

8 Srinagar

9 Srinagar

10 Srinagar — Gulmarg

11 Gulmarg — Nagin Lake

12 Nagin Lake

13 Srinagar

August 14 Fly: Srinagar - Delhi

15 Delhi

16 Delhi

17 Delhi

18 Delhi - Tansen, Nepal

19 Tansen - Pokara

20 Pokara

21 Pokara

22 Pokara - Katmandu

23 Katmandu

24 Katmandu

25 Katmandu

26 Katmandu - Varanasi

27 Varanasi

28 Varanasi

29 Agra

August 30 Agra

31 Jaipur

Sept 1 Jaipur - Delhi

2 Delhi

3 Delhi

4 Delhi

5 Fly: Delhi - London

6 London

7 Train: London - Frankfurt

8 Fly: Frankft - SEATTLE

Good trip - thats all
I got to say.

56 days
10 countries
countless miles
gillions of experiences
and memories

Rick Steves
Gene Openshaw
9/8/78

Preface (2022)

Back in the 1970s, the ultimate trip for any backpacker was the so-called "Hippie Trail" from Istanbul to Kathmandu. Travelers knew Europe was just the wading pool for world exploration, and this tantalizing adventure awaited just to the east. By 1978 I had spent five summers since high school graduation exploring Europe and was aching to turn in my Eurail Pass for a dive into the deep end…to venture beyond "the West."

But it was scary. For two years I had plans, even ticket reservations…but then found an excuse to put off India and do Europe again. Then, upon graduation from college—and with the right travel partner (my buddy Gene Openshaw, who joined me the day after high school graduation in 1973 on our first big Europe trip)—everything aligned for the trek from Europe to Nepal through Turkey, Iran, Afghanistan, and India. And we did it.

This was two years before I wrote my first book, Europe Through the Back Door. In 1978, I expected to be a piano teacher all my life…a piano teacher who traveled in the summer. I journaled like a travel writer in training, penning 60,000 words while doing the Hippie Trail, then flew home and dove into adulthood. In the wake of this adventure, I made a decision that changed the trajectory of my young life: I let my piano students go, turned my recital hall into a lecture hall, and became what people who hire me for speaking engagements insist on calling me: a travel guru.

In 1978, this journal was packed away, never read…forgotten for 42 years. Then, with the pandemic in 2020, I dug it out, had it transcribed, and as if on an anthropological dig into my own past, I entered the world of a 23-year-old me and relived my coming-of-age trip.

Editing this into something more polished and mature is not an option. This journal is stream-of-consciousness honesty—a candid, unvarnished snapshot of my world and my outlook in 1978. While the text has been lightly edited for spelling and clarity, I was careful not to make me older or wiser or more culturally sensitive than I was at the time.

Ready for the adventure of a lifetime? Stow away with me now as we meet a 23-year-old who, not knowing where life would take him, teamed up with a buddy to travel from Europe to Kathmandu. Enjoy the road.

Words can't explain my joy as I stepped across that happy tree-lined border. I dreamed so long to experience this enchanted sub-continent and now I knew I was her... I endured the overland road ... many moments, long moments, ... idea was a stupid mist... fun + foo... I could ... now as I walked ... after buffa... and lush ... earning wit... a feeling ... it soared. I doubt ... way again bu... I experienced three ... x unforgettable week and learned so much about many different peoples and alot about myself, I've turned the key and the world opened up before me, rekindling the flame that Europe was beginning to have trouble w...

After clearing customs we hopped into a mini bus for Amritsar. Before long it was packed to the hilt and I knew this was India. I liked it.

Amritsar, just across the border from Lahore, is the capital of the Punjab, the holy center of the Sikh religion and a jumbly city full of frantic bicycle rickshaws and people. We checked into the Tourist Guest House and got a large no frills double with a fan for $2 or 20 rs. Gene was still gloomy + feeling lousy so he sacked out while I went out to arrange for our ticket to Kashmir. There was little point in walking when I could get doorstep service in the rickshaws for pennies. I sat in the buggy part while a hard working but very eager guy happily peddaled me where ever I wanted to go.

We wanted to fly to Srinagar to save many hours of hassels + travel time. There were no flights available for several days so rather despe... tickets. ... sleep but we also needed to get up to Srinagar. I grab...

As a backpacker, I never traveled without writing, diligent and daily, in my journal.

Friday, July 14, 1978: Frankfurt

Nineteen hundred and seventy-eight is the big year. At least, I feel like I am doing something big. Having finished school after 18 seemingly endless years, the end did come. The University of Washington was great… but I didn't bother to go to the graduation ceremony. I was so ready to move on. But I couldn't imagine what would follow. It just felt right to take a trip—a long one.

I believe that a trip is a noble adventure and a wise investment of time and money, but maybe I just have nothing better to do with my time and money. Life in Seattle is good—but for no more than nine months out of twelve.

Of all things to waste, time is the worst, and on the road, even wasted time is time well spent. The comfort of Europe has long been the answer to my fear of a wasted summer at home. But after eight trips, Europe is losing much of its magnetism and, refusing to accept the fact, it took one final six-week trip on "the continent" to prove to me that it is time for something new. Europe is a well-worn pair of shoes—very comfortable—but as a traveler, I need more… something to whack my norms.

India has burned in my heart for years. For a few years, I made plans but found excuses to cancel and just do Europe again. I think I was afraid. Finally, the plans have been made, and that's where I am heading. Wide-eyed anticipation of totally new cultures, unforgettable experiences, exposure to life from a bizarre and almost exotic angle is stoking my wanderlust. An acceptance of the frustration, sweat, sickness, sleepless nights, fears, and hardships is an integral part of this package deal. A package deal that no one else can open. Only I can have it…and only by traveling through it.

The road to India is a long one. The pavement stops with Europe—but that's where the drive becomes a ride animated by inconceivably exciting potholes. Like a skier craves moguls, I need India.

The road actually began 36 hours ago, wrapping up my annual Europe trip in Helsinki. After a smooth ride by boat and train, I arrived as planned in Frankfurt, aiming to pick up my friend Gene and carry on to Bulgaria.

Nothing was more important to me today than meeting up with Gene. Five years ago, Gene and I "did Europe" in crazy style starting the day after graduating from high school. In the meantime, Gene graduated from Stanford (Comparative Religious Studies) and I from the University of Washington (European History and Business Admin), and now we plan on picking up where we left off at the Frankfurt airport, this time leaving Europe and heading east.

For six weeks this summer, I have traveled Europe from Italy to Finland, too often in the company of loneliness or someone who was little better. The trip taught me the value of good people and how the value of good things is enhanced when shared with good people. India is a good thing. Gene is "good people." The table is set…and I'm hungry.

Gene's plane landed at 9:10, and I was there waiting. Somehow, we missed each other as I witnessed every reunion except my own. What a frustrating feeling to watch that electric door open a hundred times and see no familiar face. Like a puppy, the door would open, I'd look for Gene, and see someone else. After an hour, I had Gene paged: "Mrs. Gene Openshaw. Paging Mrs. Gene Openshaw." It sounded funny to hear Gene paged as "Mrs." With no sign of him, bad thoughts traveled through my mind. What if he didn't make the plane? What if something happened? Terrible! What if I was destined to spend the next eight weeks alone? While fighting with my optimism, tail between my legs, I returned to Frankfurt's train station to the backup meeting place—lucky Track 13. And that's where Gene was waiting for me.

For some reason, the trains to Yugoslavia required reservations, and most were sold out. We got a 5:00 p.m. ticket to Belgrade (about $80 Frankfurt to Belgrade, second class), and now had the day to blow in Frankfurt. Neither of us was in a European-sightseeing mood, so it was more of a frolic day just bounc-

---

Top left: Rick and Gene in school. Right: Gene joined me in 1973 for a whirlwind Europe tour just after high school graduation. That trip was a kind of warm up for 1978. Bottom left: Rick and Gene, after 40 years, still good travel buddies.

ing around big, modern, but not-bad Frankfurt. Jimmy Carter will be in town tomorrow morning, but hopefully by then we'll be in Yugoslavia.

We hopped off the train for the evening in Wurzburg (it's great how tickets let you hop on and off), and it just happened to be during a beer festival… kind of a mini-Oktoberfest. (It was as if we'd planned it.) Festivals are great fun even if you spend no money. The huge, packed beer hall was livened by a brassy band and lots of beer.

Twenty-three years after the end of WWII, Germany is still full of US soldiers and their families. It's a bad scene with lousy pay and little off-base discipline. A military policeman bought us a beer if we'd listen to his story. He can't win. "Break up a fight, and you get cussed out by both parties—even the guy who was getting his face beat in."

Outside, the rides and games whirled ceaselessly. There was a blonde German girl who must have just stepped out of a dream…in both of our 23-year-old brains. While it might have been kind of creepy, we just tracked her around for a couple hours. I'll never forget that goddess spinning in the big barrel in the sky.

At 10:30 that night, we hopped into a train and left Germany, heading south and east.

It's only day two, in Bulgaria, and, realizing "we can't even read the letters here," it occurs to us that we're really in for an adventure. In the 40 years since, Gene and I have co-authored about a dozen guidebooks and two books about European art.

Saturday, July 15: Germany to Belgrade

All night and all day were spent on the train. We spent a crowded night not sleeping very well—for some reason, the rhythm of the rails—which I normally enjoy—was a steady annoying drum roll. At least we had good seats. This was my fourth night in a row sleeping—or at least attempting to sleep—on a train (since Savonlinna, Finland). While the sleep was rotten, I liked the cost (free with my train pass) and the efficiency of traveling at night to have days free to actually do things.

In an effort to let Gene stretch out and catch some elusive sleep, I went into the aisle to lay down on the floor. The plan didn't work, for in a few minutes, the ticket collector told me to get up and then discovered Gene was sold the wrong ticket route through Austria. After some heated discussion, we saw no alternative than to pay the extra $14 owed, and by now, it was 5:00 a.m., light, and the night was gone.

Even through sleepy eyes, the lush Austrian countryside was enough to make you stand by the window. The ride through Austria was punctuated by nibbling, snoozing, and taking in the views. Leaning just a little out an open train window adds a dash of danger to the mix. By noon, the Yugoslavian customs official had two American passports in his office, and I waited outside with

the touched-up photo of Tito (the country's dictator's photos made him look impossibly smooth) looking over me. Big Daddy is everywhere in this country. (And what does he use for his skin!?) Passports stamped and in my pocket, I felt a surge of travel enthusiasm, splashed my face awake, jogged around a bit, and boarded the train, celebrating the fact that we were two-thirds of the way to Belgrade, halfway to Sofia, and nowhere near India.

Now the day was young, and 12 hours had to pass. The Yugoslavian countryside is rather dull. The most entertaining site is the peasant families working together with the scarecrows in the fields. The time passed, as it always does, and we read, played backgammon on Gene's mini-board, ate, and snoozed. When sleeping on the train sitting up, my head just bobs like Gumby in the breeze. While dead asleep, sooner or later, my aching neck wakes me up. I hoped I wouldn't grow a hunch from slouching while sleeping less than "bolt upright" through the many long rides between here and India.

The best thing about traveling with someone is you have a chance to talk, and I seemed to be making up for lost time. Talking with Gene—of my trip, girls, life directions, big decisions, and old friends—seemed to speed the train along.

Dinner was highlighted by bread and cheese, cabbage, and warm milk that somehow doesn't spoil (pity). Boxed milk here is sold bragging that it needs no refrigeration and will never go bad. (It'll never go good either.) Running an hour late, the train pulled into Belgrade at 10:00 p.m.

We both knew we deserved a bed and, after buying tickets to Sofia ($16), we set out with $4 in local money, knowing we'd find nothing that cheap. The chase for sleep began with hotels (too expensive), private pensions (still too much), the parks (perfectly within our budgets). Belgrade was crawling with policemen, complete with machine guns, patrolling the parks, and after an uneasy hour trying to scavenge some sleep in the park, it became clear we weren't going to find a secluded, dark, and safe-feeling corner to lie down in. So, we packed up and returned to the train station.

We decided to find a train car that was going nowhere and sack out in it. We did, and there were plenty of others with the same idea inside. Within moments we had found the sleep we craved.

Kabam! Lurching forward, the unthinkable happened. Our train jolted into motion and, suddenly, was going somewhere! Fast as possible, we woke, packed, and watched helplessly as the lights of downtown Belgrade faded and the train lumbered through the night. It slowed for a small station just outside town, and thinking now-or-never, I tossed my bag before me and then jumped out. Gene followed, but the train had picked up speed, and he tumbled wildly into the dark, deserted cement platform. Rushing to his side and hoping he was ok, I helped him up, and we surveyed the situation. Happily, bruises and scuffs were the only results.

We had barely started our adventure, and I was haunted by the thought that, in our haste, we could have easily jumped out of the train and hit a pillar on the platform, which would have bounced us back on the moving train. We both agreed that leaving the park to find peace and safety on a lonely train and then dying like that would have been a good example of irony.

The lone station master, flashlight in hand, came over to inspect the American teenagers who had just dropped into his sleepy station…from a train that didn't stop. Pitying us, he let us sleep in the waiting room there and, after all that crazy adventure to find a place to lay my head, I was not about to turn down this literally concrete offer for a safe, warm, and free night's sleep.

Sunday, July 16: Belgrade

Early that morning, we returned to Belgrade and spent an hour or so browsing around town. Then we were back at the station, this time catching a train that was actually going somewhere…and somewhere we wanted to go: Bulgaria.

A panic overcame me a few minutes before the train was scheduled to leave. I didn't know where it was in this chaotic Belgrade central station. Scrambling frantically to find the right track, we found it was late, and there was suddenly no need to panic. Sitting there, two hours passed, and I didn't really mind—I knew this was only the beginning of a very long journey.

At about 11:00, the 9:30 train arrived. And, after shuffling on board, it became evident that there were no seats left. We found a spot in the aisle with a fold-down stool and a good window. (When a train is full in Europe, there is always a fold-down "seat" in the aisle—which, while little bigger than the fold-down "table" on the back of an airplane seat, I actually kind of like.) This would be our home for the day.

Our last Yugoslavian coins were spent on cookies. We had a liter of milk (which never goes bad/good), and everything was set. A Turk had moved in piles of suitcases and boxes, cutting our little spot way down but providing us with a marvelous table. The train rolled out, and we cracked open the food. Americans are very finicky about germs, and it must have been funny here in Serbia to watch us place the tablecloth down carefully and keep everything as

clean and orderly as possible. Then I punched a small hole in the milk and asked Gene to hold it. As he grabbed it, milk spurted like a geyser out the top and all over me. Everyone enjoyed us—as if we were two comedians on the train. I wiped off my glasses and got down to my milk and cookies.

To save a few bucks, I purchased tickets only to Sofia, planning to fake our way a few hours farther to Plovdiv. The border crossing was typically hassled, but after the stern Yugoslav police made way for stern Bulgarian police, we were successfully one layer deeper into the Communist world. Welcome to Bulgaria.

Sofia, the capital, came and went, and now we, sitting on the big Turkish suitcase, were riding farther than our ticket covered us—stowing away—playing backgammon and hoping they wouldn't have tickets checked until Plovdiv came, and we could hop out of the rolling scene of our petty crime.

But luck was not ours, and tension mounted as the conductor neared. We went over our options and decided to fake like we still believed we were going to Sofia and didn't realize we had passed it. Relishing my role as the stupid American tourist, I really played it up. Oh, how I was upset and determined to get to Sofia tonight for my hotel. It took forever for the conductor and half the people on the train to explain to us that Sofia was now behind us. The conductor saw a golden opportunity to cash in on this and was trying to charge $25, but I was too distraught…upset about missing my hotel in Sofia. Finally, the train man began to think this whole mess was funny and, after much sweet-talking, he accepted $4 from us, providing we promised to get off at the next stop—Plovdiv. I wanted to tell some of the Europeans who got involved that Americans aren't really that stupid, but I never got a chance. But I did get a chance to receive an imaginary Oscar for my acting from Gene.

For me, Bulgaria is just one family living in its historic second city (Plovdiv). And I make a point to visit about once a year. The family: Svetoslav (Sveti); his younger sister, Virginia; mom; dad; and grandmother. Their endearing terms for each other: Miko (mother), Datko (father), Botko (brother), and Siko (sister). They are my window on the East, and I am their window on the West. And, as the West is mysterious and forbidden, for Svetoslav and his freedom-starved family, my annual visits were treasured. While they were forbidden to enjoy much of our culture—music, movies, TV—and dreamed of traveling there, the capitalist West was, for the typical Bulgarian, something they would neither understand nor ever visit. We had to be very sneaky as they were not allowed to have Western guests.

Plovdiv came, and we stepped off the train, hoping to be met by a familiar face. Seeing nothing but a few uniformed soldiers and the typical busy, but strangely quiet, station crowd, we left the station thinking maybe Svetoslav or his father would be in front. Seeing nothing, I studied the map and set out to find their address. On a quiet, dark street, taking long steps to pass an old lady, we felt the tense excitement of being the forbidden fruit in a socialistic country. Then a voice broke the rhythm of the footsteps: "Rick! Rick!" I knew exactly who that was. I told Gene, "Keep a low profile and walk quickly." We followed Svetoslav until, finally, we felt safe. Then Svetoslav's warm handshake couldn't begin to express our happiness to be together again.

Datko waited nearby in their "Polsky Fiat" (a cheap communist car made in Poland from worn-out factory parts, sold cheap by the Italian company). He couldn't speak English, but that wasn't necessary. Datko and I, together for the fourth summer in a row, could communicate without English. Leaving our rucksacks in the car, we entered the apartment, and a happy reunion was waiting. Along with Datko and Sveti, Miko, Siko, and Grandma were all there just like last year.

Security had to be tight. To have Western guests, especially overnight, is a serious offense in Bulgaria. The packs were left in the car because it would be foolish to let snoopy neighbors see the luggage of Western visitors being brought into their flat. After a nice meal and catching up, we went over to Grandma's place to sleep in peace. (Less risk of betrayal by neighbors.)

Our first priority: showers and laundry. Then Botko played his new Beatles album that I brought over until it was past everyone's bedtime.

Monday, July 17: Plovdiv

This day was for relaxing and just enjoying everyone's company. No one had any big plans, and that made the day beautiful. After sleeping in and eating a big brunch, there was a good conversation and trading of news. Since Botko can't leave his country, he enjoys cultivating friends from around the world to bring that forbidden fruit to him. Inflation, unemployment, Jimmy Carter, relative wages and prices, and lifestyles were discussed. He dreams of travel to the West, gobbles up anything he can get his hands on about the Capitalist world, and, while he's never been there, he knows London better than I do.

A walk around old and new Plovdiv, a special dinner, and a French movie finished off the day. Then, back at Grandma's, we climbed under our Albanian-made blankets (the first thing we had ever seen that had been in or out of that mysterious place) and slept very well—after a bottle of Coke and some Beatles, of course. In 1978 Bulgaria, Coke and Beatles are the tickets to an amazing time.

Last summer, I learned what had special value in Bulgaria, and this year, I was determined to bring it in. I asked Gene to buy and shuttle over the latest hot items: a Texas Instruments calculator ($12), Swabbies jeans ($12), Scotch recording tape ($8), and a Beatles album ($8). These things, totaling $40 in value, most Americans can earn in one day. Their value in Bulgaria, Eastern Europe, and the USSR is incredible. For a Bulgarian (average wage is 150 leva a month, or about $150), the calculator is worth 130 leva, jeans 30 leva, recording tape 30 leva, Beatles album 30 leva, totaling 210 leva, or about six-weeks wages for a factory worker in Bulgaria. It made me feel very good to give such valuable presents—as I'm usually not a great gift-giver.

Plovdiv has been fixed up to be a lovely city. Wide, clean, pleasant walking malls are lined by typical socialist-type stores. Only the government can advertise, and it exercises that right liberally, going through tons of red paint. A military band plays patriotic and folk songs in the park. People stroll and troll. Next to the fountain, men gather to discuss sports—especially soccer. They argue and argue, ignoring the plainclothes policeman in their midst who monitors their discussion, while making sure everything remains apolitical.

Datko bought us ice cream and Schweppes tonic water while we struggled to spend our Bulgarian money, which will be worthless once we leave the country.

Botko had always wanted to hear me play the piano, and now he had his chance. Dropping by the local Mr. Music, we enjoyed guitars, a trumpet, and a good organ complete with rhythm box. This man did all the teaching, conducting, and so on for the school, and he had lots of stuff to play with, including the

Svetoslav, his father, and Gene. Entertaining Westerners in your home was a dangerous move in communist Bulgaria.

popular records—Santana, Jesus Christ Superstar, and Uriah Heep. While an organ is not a piano, I got my chance and had some fun making music.

Capitalists in Bulgaria are treated to special prices. Traveling as a capitalist in a socialist country can be costly. The price of everything from hotels and train rides to amusement-park games goes up. To make matters worse, the official exchange rate is about four times worse than the actual value of the dollar. I shot four bullets in a marksmanship game and foolishly gave a 2-leva bill to pay for it. I expected a bill for 40 stotinki but got only 80 stotinki back. I was charged 90 minutes of a factory wage to shoot those four bullets because I was a money-grubbing capitalist. Datko called to find the price of a ticket to Istanbul—$11. When I tried to buy it, the price had increased to $16.

The summer theater was open, and everyone was going to see the Louis de Funès movie. "But Botko, we don't speak French or Bulgarian." "It's ok, just his face will make you laugh." It did. Siko translated for Gene and Botko for me, and all had a good laugh. Movies are very popular in Bulgaria. Western ones are always sold out. Sveti explained how Russian movies are great to take your girlfriend to. "The theater is dark and empty, and you can kiss for two hours without missing a thing."

The Godfather and *Love Story* both opened in Sofia but were censored—shut down after a few days—and will not be shown again. Some things are just not fit for human eyes—or minds.

Tuesday, July 18: Plovdiv

Today was our last day in Bulgaria, and it was a busy one. On the way from granny's to Datko's, Botko took us to the top of the hill for a panorama and to check out the monument to the "liberation of 1945." (Cynics say, "Ya, liberation from Hitler to Stalin.") Then it was time for brunch, followed by a trip to the countryside to see Bachkovo Monastery and some small towns. I had been here three years ago with my girlfriend, Ruth, but it had since been restored, and it was even better a second time around. The frescos were wonderfully colorful! Then, after dinner and some last conversation and time together, the train was actually on time (very rare), and we all had to hustle on down to the station to say goodbye. The long night, which would come with a touchy border crossing, had begun, and soon we would be in Istanbul.

The meals in Plovdiv made us feel like kings. Hospitality flowed in many forms, and the most tangible was food. Each day usually had two big meals. A typical lunch would be a salad, cold meat and cheeses, bread, Coke, soup, and hot milk, which instant coffee and sugar were stirred into. For dinner, there

Lamb's head...In Bulgaria there's nothing but the best for out-of-town guests.

was more of the same with possibly stuffed peppers, hot pork chops, boiled potatoes, and wine or a local liquor.

At a restaurant near Bachkovo Monastery, Datko treated everyone to lamb's head. I thought this must be a real delicacy, but it's actually quite common. To explain why there's such an abundance of lamb's heads, Datko shared a little politics, joking about how Bulgaria gets only the leftovers, as it seems their best production is exported to the USSR. He asked (according to Sveti's translation), "What's the biggest animal in the world?" I had no idea. Datko then said, "The Bulgarian lamb—its body is in the USSR, and its head is in Bulgaria."

As if on cue with our laughter, the lamb's heads—four of them—were brought in: eyelashes, teeth, eyeballs, and all. And there they sat, just staring at me and Gene. We didn't know what to do but take pictures. Then it was time to learn how to eat them. The tongue and eyeballs were supposed to be best. The brain was hard to swallow, but Botko was happy to take any leftovers. Actually, the lamb's head made a fun meal, and I ripped off some teeth for souvenirs. But, while I was away from the table, the waiter cleared them off.

The beer was Czechoslovakian and good. Everyone in Eastern Europe reaches for the Czech beer when they have the option. The local Plovdiv beer comes in a bare bottle, and that means the beer is bad.

Knowing how international trains lumbering through Bulgaria are generally quite late, we were all counting on the train being two hours or so late so we could have a good last evening together. But, sadly, the train was on time. Datko called from the station, shared the bad news, and we had to hurry. We gathered together all our stuff, plus the wonderful goodies bag Miko prepared for us for our long journey. Then we all hustled down to the station.

It's always difficult to leave Plovdiv. The last waving sight of that wonderful Bulgarian family outside the train window is so dramatic and heart-warming. Before finding seats, we stopped in the aisle, slammed down our window, and waved, and waved, and waved…waiting for the train to roll us away. This was the last oasis. From now on, we were on our own. Heading east from Bulgaria, it occurred to me that I knew no one between here and the USA… more than half a world away.

For many, a train ride meant standing in the aisle for hours.

We found a room with only three men in it but getting in was a challenge. The Turk closest to the door refused to get up and said that he had three friends who were in the bathroom who had the vacant seats and the compartment was full. The two other men, Iranians, were ready to let us in and apologized for the Turk. We enjoyed the view out the aisle window, had a good conversation with two Iraqis for about an hour, and then broke in on the comfortable threesome. Like sardines, everyone made themselves as comfortable as possible. One thought lurked in every mind—the Bulgaria-Turkey border crossing.

This was my fourth Turko-Bulgarian border crossing. Each one was in the middle of the night and very, very long. The train just stopped, and one man after another would walk through with some bureaucratic duty to do. The Americans' bags weren't even touched, but the poor Iranians had everything sifted through and had to pay a curious tax of two new shirts to one official.

For us, things couldn't have gone smoother, and with the first light of the new day, we were into Turkey, free from the hassles of socialist Bulgaria and falling into the arms of Turkish chaos.

CHAPTER 2

All Aboard the Pirate's Bus: Turkey to Iran

July 19–23

Wednesday, July 19: Istanbul

I actually slept through the morning and felt rested upon arrival in crazy Istanbul. Today was for business—change money, buy a bus ticket to Tehran, get an Iranian visa, find a hotel. Feeling right at home, I walked up to my favorite street and checked into my regular hotel, Agan Hotel. A little bit cocky, I expected people to remember me since I remembered them. I didn't even check out the room, I just took it, confident that it would be as good as last year's. It wasn't.

Istanbul life just carries on—day after day, the same dusty human packhorses, the same small boys selling Marlborough cigarettes, the same go-easy guys sitting on piles of tires. Just walking around is an experience, and you can't help but become swallowed up in the earthy atmosphere.

Changing money was a challenge since most banks wouldn't accept traveler's checks. The nice thing was that, for a change, we could enjoy a much-improved exchange rate. Last year the dollar bought only 16 lira. Now it's good for 25! That makes Turkey fantastically cheap.

We had to buy a ticket to Tehran. We expected to pay $15-$20, but the cheapest bus around was 800 lira, or $32. Oh well—that's halfway to India. We went to the most highly recommended company, Mihan Tours, which advertised: "Big new Mercedes buses—very comfortable." We booked good seats—numbers 21 and 22 on what promised to be a lovely bus. This was a two-day bus ride, and comfort was of the utmost importance. We felt confident that we were with the right company—they were so smooth and business-like.

Istanbul is a sprawling city, part in Asia and part in Europe. Where east meets west, it's the kickoff point for the Hippie Trail to Kathmandu.

Wandering the streets of Istanbul can be endlessly entertaining.

Now, with our chores taken care of, we were free to enjoy the sights of Istanbul. We visited the Blue Mosque where I saw the same old guy with no legs selling postcards who warmed the steps last year. We saw a British guy we had met in Belgrade, treated ourselves to some sütlaç (rice pudding) and cherry juice, and then went back to our hotel to relax.

The room was simply lousy. The toilet didn't flush, the shower only trickled, the lights didn't work, and cockroaches flourished. My shoes earned a new nickname: "the roach-stompers." You just stomp and drag across the rug leaving only a dark smudge—a fate too good for any cockroach found in my hotel room. We called for help and what we got was a new room…just the same except the lights worked.

Rested and ready to go for an evening stroll, we plunged into the Turkish bustle, wide-eying our way down to the waterfront. I can't get enough of Istanbul's churning, busy waterfront. Gene bought fried fish and a hunk of bread right off a little cooking dingy, and a joyful Turk gave us each a breadstick. The Galata Bridge was full of cute Turkish girls—still giggly in their 20s. Climbing up through the "new town," we passed a street soccer game and reached the top of the hill where we ascended the Galata Tower for a fantastic view of the Golden Horn, Bosphorus, and an Istanbul—with sprawling millions of people where Asia meets Europe—that I didn't even know existed.

The sun set, and we returned to our hotel to rest, have a bite of Miko's Bulgarian cake, and stomp a few roaches. I intended to go back outside, but after a shower, I was so comfortable on the bed I never got back up. At least until about 3:00 a.m., when our toilet began to overflow again.

Thursday, July 20: Istanbul

Breakfast was great. We went to my favorite little omelet shop. The guy didn't remember me, but he remembered how to make my omelet. That with my favorites—rice pudding and cherry fruit juice—made a good breakfast. Next, we took in our passports to get an Iranian visa, and I let Gene check out the bazaar alone while I was very lazy back at the hotel.

When you're in such an intense and high-pressure environment, your body enjoys a chance to just be quiet.

The early afternoon was spent simply wandering about aimlessly—letting ourselves be swallowed up into the bustle of Istanbul. After being disappointed by our watermelon that was white and an unappetizing yellow inside, we made our way back to our neighborhood and stepped into the Turkish hamam, or bath, for that Turkish spa experience that we'd promised ourselves.

A complete Turkish bath and a massage is an experience everyone should have, and no one can forget. Feeling really naked (we had to leave everything, including our money belts, in the little booth), wrapped only with a towel, we were led into the same steamy world I experienced last year. My unshaven

---

Back before the internet, travelers communicated and teamed up using message boards at gathering spots like Istanbul's Pudding Shop. Wanna buy a cheap Vanagon? The manager at the Pudding Shop still serves up my favorite dish in Turkey: sütlaç (rice pudding).

Turk said, "okay, merhaba," and put me onto the big round marble slab where I was allowed to lie, sweat, look up at the cloudy sun rays spraying through the little holes in the domed roof, and worry about the body-ripping massage I was about to get. I prayed that my joints would all survive.

Then with a loud slap in my chest, he landed on me and worked me over good. He was a credit to his gender. Smashing and stretching each of my tight muscles, I was in lovely pain. It hurt but, in a strange way, I wanted it—just with no lasting damage. Then came the joint stretching. He flipped me over, face down. Bouncing my feet to my back, walking on me, cracking my neck with surely enough power to break it, I'd call the massage an all-out attack. At one point, I realized my left cheek and ear were pressed against the wet marble with the rest of my body at the mercy of my masseuse and, a few feet in front of me was Gene, all wrapped up in the same agonizing pretzel, right cheek and ear pressed against the wet marble. We were providing the whole ordeal with a soundtrack of constant grunting and groaning.

After this, they washed and scrubbed us by a hot fountain. We were relieved to be uninjured and totally relaxed now. But the mood of this phase was destroyed by their concern for how much we would pay them. We were trying to relax and get into it, and they were jabbering away about money, money, money.

Back in our booth, we happily found our valuables untouched. We dried off and dressed, deciding that under no circumstances would we pay more than 100 lira (or $4 each) for the whole thing. Not without problems, we got away for 90 lira each.

Feeling clean and good, we knew this wouldn't last. We checked out of our hotel room, organized and cleaned our packs—discovering that our supply of precious Ziploc bags had been stolen—and walked out to catch our bus to Tehran.

Well, we were ready and optimistic about the long ride ahead of us. In 63 hours, we planned to be in Tehran, Iran.

Knowing we had seats 21 and 22, we saw no reason to rush on. We took our breakables and what we'd need for the journey into our day bags and heaved our rucksacks to the man standing on top of the bus. They disappeared under a canvas. Last on, we soon realized that seat reservations were worthless on this bus.

We took what was left—the last two seats that were built onto the back of the last row of normal seats over the rear stairwell. They collapsed forward when someone came in the rear entrance but didn't recline back like the others for sleeping. We bounced slowly out of Istanbul at about 6:30, and, taking stock of the situation, we found little to cheer about. The driver looked like a crazy Barbary pirate, complete with hairy open chest, mustache, and bandana. The #2 man was a half-wit with grotesque pockmarks disfiguring his face. Our window didn't open and was covered with old, dirty eagle decals. The wheel

Above: Our seats were folded out over the stairwell in the back of the bus...and unlike every other seat on the bus, they didn't recline. Right: We called our bus driver "The Pirate" and our very survival was in his hands.

casing just in front of us cut down legroom and made the ride extra noisy and bouncy. The engine just behind us was hot, smelled, and rumbled constantly. Our reading lights didn't work, my seat came complete with a sharp point and nasty, exposed screw. Cigarette ashes blew straight into me from nearby smokers, and the cover of the aisle light crashed to the floor just as we crossed the bridge over the Bosphorus and entered Asia. Cuss this tour bus. Only 62 hours to go. We passed time expertly, playing word games, trivia, telling stories, having heavy discussions, and reading and singing old songs.

Then when it was time to think about sleeping, we cracked open our Bulgarian gift of cognac. At first, I hated the powerful stuff, but I grew bolder and bolder. The Iranians gave us several big glasses of Scotch to speed us along. We finished the whole bottle of cognac and were so drunk I couldn't believe it. I never enjoyed a night bus ride in seats that didn't recline so much. When we had finished off everything, Gene had to take a pee. I'll never forget him filling, actually over-filling, the cognac bottle in the crazy back seat of that crazy bus. We screwed the cap back on, put it in the garbage, and slept like babies as we rumbled through Turkey.

Friday, July 21: Bus from Kayseri to Sivas, Turkey

The "pirate" (as we called our driver) suddenly started screaming. I snapped awake just as the half-wit driver was grinding us over the curb and crashing the bus to a noisy stop. Smoke billowed out from our end of the bus. I thought we were on fire and, before we stopped, thoughts of how terrible this could be raced through my woozy head.

Things went flying everywhere, but luckily the human luggage stayed put, and everyone was ok. The pock-faced half-wit had just taken over and couldn't have been driving for more than a minute when he lost control, and we crashed through the meridian curb. We all filed out to inspect the damage as the cold Anatolian wind blew fiercely. The bus didn't look too bad, but it was hung up on the two-foot-high curb, and we spent the next hour building rock bridges so our Iranian leaders could work the bus out of this jam. Slowly it rocked back onto the road, and we limped into the next town to get it fixed.

No one thought this would be a quick stop. The pirate was screaming at the half-wit, Turkish grease monkeys climbed under the rear end, small boys brought tea and bread rings, and I found a place free of animal crap to stretch out and get some more sleep.

With smoke, sparks, and screams, I was jolted awake as our bus ran off the road and ground to a halt. We spent the better part of a day hanging out while the bus was repaired.

The sun warmed me to sleep, only to be woken up an hour later. We were all taken to the technical school to relax, and friendly men there did their best to make us comfortable.

The next six hours were spent drinking tea, snoozing, washing under a hose, and getting to know the rest of the people on the bus. By now, it became apparent—this was to be no 63-hour ride, but we were beginning an odyssey. One which no one knew the outcome. We would just ride it out.

Finally, the pirate yelled what must have been "all aboard" in Turkish, and we continued eastward. The bus was filled with an interesting group of people. The four Iranian crew members were wild and crazy, and, as we had seen, only one could drive a bus. He would be doing the rest of the long haul alone, so we were in for a much longer ride than anticipated. Gene and I were the only Americans and, compared to everyone else, I think we seemed quite green to this kind of travel. Four or five British, two Belgian, four or five French, a couple of

Top: Each night, gathered with bus mates in unforgettable hotels, we considered our situation. Bottom: Every day, we'd unfold our map and see how we were getting farther and farther from our comfort zone...and still nowhere near Kathmandu.

Basques, a rotund Russian emigre living in Chicago, an Iranian student, some Muslim women with children, and a few others rounded out the bus.

It was nearly 3:00 now, and we drove through spectacular high country, not making very good time. The roads were bad, our pace was slow, and by late that night, we were only by Sivas—far from Erzurum, which is halfway to Tehran. Stopping at a village, the driver and his cronies took their time over dinner and got involved in a Henry Fonda movie that was babbling away on Turkish TV. He said we were staying here and found a hotel for some people. Gene and I were put with the two Belgians in a prison-like, four-bedded room. At least it was clean. We slept from 1:00 to 6:30 while those who remained on the bus had a terrible night dealing with the half-wit, horny Turks, and corrupt police looking for trouble.

Saturday, July 22: Sivas to Erzurum

Rudely awakened for the second morning in a row, I was shrieked out of bed by the crazy pirate and scolded all the way back to the waiting bus. It was nearly 7:00, and we had been told we were leaving at 5:00. I was nearly hurled by my hair as I got in but managed a cheery "good morning" to the gang on board. After half an hour, we made our first stop, a lengthy one, and we knew that today our tyrannical driver was in no hurry. After breakfast, the road got bad, and we were still far from Erzurum.

At mid-morning, we stopped by a riverside, and the pirate stripped to his underpants and, with soap in hand, he went for a bath and swim. Like a wild kid, he rolled in the sand and reentered the river. Then he urged everyone on, saying, "No bath, no Tehran." We were slow to catch on, but soon all the men were running around in our underpants and floating down the refreshing river. It felt great. I washed me and my dusty clothes and dried off in minutes.

By now, we had given up hope of any great progress today and figured we'd be sleeping in Erzurum tonight, and our driver was just going to enjoy himself along the way.

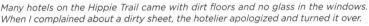

Many hotels on the Hippie Trail came with dirt floors and no glass in the windows. When I complained about a dirty sheet, the hotelier apologized and turned it over.

An American was big news in eastern Turkey. When people stared, I assumed they were waiting for entertainment. So, I'd sing. (My go-to was "Huggin' and Chalkin'" by Hoagy Carmichael.)

By 3:00, we were in Erzurum, halfway to Tehran. Our packs were thrown down from the roof, and we were told to find a hotel and report back at 4:00 tomorrow morning—not 5:00.

Our no-frills, 35-lira room became the meeting place for the English-speaking part of our bus. The mood was a helpless and pessimistic frustration. We shared some food and wondered what the rest of the road to India would be like, and if our driver and crew would take us all the way to Tehran without any funny business—like asking for more money.

We wandered about Erzurum for a few hours, checking out a lovely mosque, lots of obnoxious people, and having a meager bite to eat. We went to bed early so we could wake up at 4:00. Our room was moderately bug-free and quiet, although there was no water anywhere, and the place was generally very filthy. We all took turns holding our noses and squatting over the little toilet. The strangest bugs gush around in the toilet bowl, and the object for anyone squatting was to "bank" things in, so nothing splashes up.

That taken care of, Gene, the two Belgians, and I all settled down and slept.

Sunday, July 23: Erzurum to Iran

We were all up and gathered in a little tea house shortly after 4:00, and by 5:00, we were underway. The pirate was determined to make good time today, and we ripped through the wild east-end of Turkey. We reached the border at about 10:00, after only a quick breakfast stop. Feeling very dominated by the boisterous Iranian bus driver, I scored a point with him by offering him a piece of our breakfast watermelon. He said, "Thank you very much. Ok! Allah! Hurry up!"

Everyone was concerned about the Turkey-Iran border crossing, and rightfully so. It is famous for drug arrests, tearing apart cars, and numerous other hassles. It's nothing to fool around with, and Gene and I checked our packs carefully to make sure that nobody had "planted" anything in them. Passing an endless line of delayed trucks, we came to the checkpoint and began the long journey through the customs building. All sorts of people were working their way across one way or the other. We filled out forms, waited for body searches that never came, and showed our passports at several points.

We thought we were done with the border as we rolled under the "Welcome to Iran" sign and passed from the omnipresent gaze of Turkey's Ataturk to that of Iran's divine Shah. Then we were stopped again and went through the luggage check. Everything was unloaded off the roof and searched. One of our wheels was even checked.

We set our clocks ahead two hours for Iran time and, by the time we were cleared for takeoff, most of the day was shot. The pirate was really moving, though. I think he wanted to get into Tehran only 24 hours late.

The Iranian countryside was dramatic and worth plenty of pictures. (With 36 shots in a roll, 14 rolls of film, and 55 days of travel, I had a limit of about 9 shots a day.) And by 10:00, we were in Tabriz just in time to witness the armored riot squads ready themselves for student trouble. Iran is quite repressive, and the students don't like that much. Torture and firing squads don't go over very well with the young generation of any country.

We all hoped we wouldn't sleep in Tabriz, where we happily said goodbye to the pock-faced half-wit. We picked up a second driver and sped straight through toward Tehran.

Now everyone's spirits picked up—this journey would be over in the morning. The Spaniards sang and clapped La Bamba, the Russian did opera, while the little smiley Iranian boy directed with a cigarette. The pirate washed his feet, sprayed everyone with rose water, made up his bed under the bus's back window, told us to shut up, and went to sleep. I waited for the night to slowly pass by—chasing sleep and checking my sluggish watch. I'm too tall for those chairs, and my neck suffers when I hang myself to sleep. I tried everything, but comfort eluded me. I did catch a few hours of sleep between tea stops. Iran will be quite different. I can tell by the truck stops—quite cheap, dull food, and crazy people.

CHAPTER 3

We're Nearly There Now—Iran

July 24-28

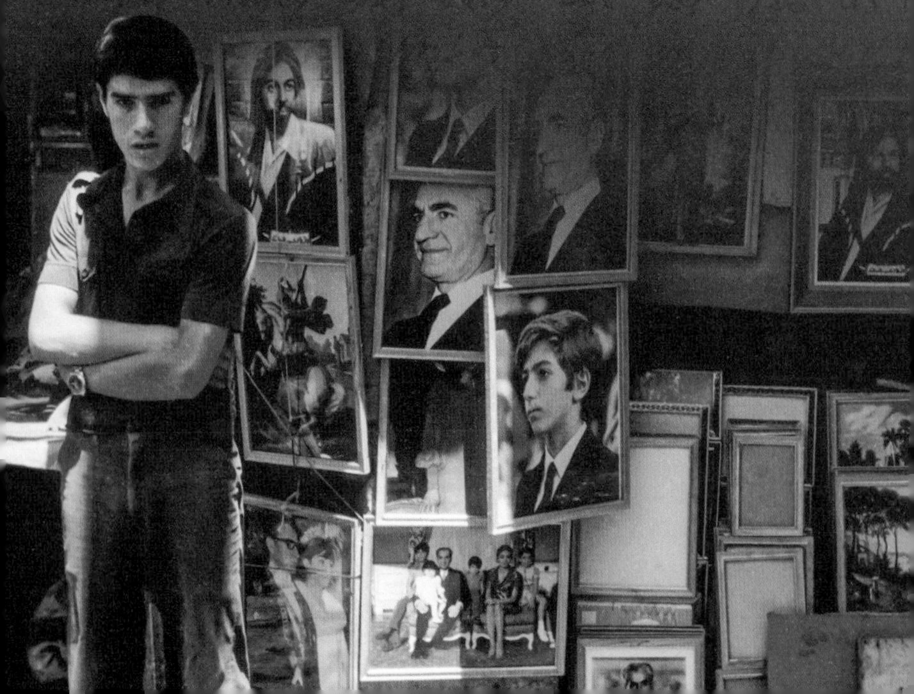

Monday, July 24: Tehran, Iran

The long night ended with the long bus ride. After four nights and three days, we had traveled from Istanbul to Tehran. That's 2,500 long kilometers (1,500 miles). Only 4,500 more kilometers (2,800 miles) to go and we'll be in Delhi!

My body from neck to tail ached but it sure felt good to get off that bus. Tehran is huge (4 million people), busy, sprawling, and very hard for me to get oriented in. We said goodbye to our bus mates, took a picture of the pirate, and set off to take care of business in Iran's capital city.

That business consisted of changing money, getting an Afghanistan visa, getting a bus ticket to Mashhad, and finding a hotel—a lot of work. Changing money was easy. We got $100 US cash for emergencies and bribes that we anticipated but hoped we wouldn't need on the road to India. The visa was easy enough. We had to leave our passports and three photos at the embassy and pick them up the next day for $7.

Now for the problem we didn't anticipate. If there was trouble, we thought it would be getting into Afghanistan. The trouble was in getting to Mashhad. Wouldn't you know it, there is a big religious festival in Iran's most holy city and we couldn't find any ride there for several days. The buses were all booked solid, the train station was chaos, and we considered flying over it or hitchhiking. Finally, as a halfway measure, we booked a bus to Gorgan, a town about halfway to Mashhad, planning to just fake our way to Mashhad from Gorgan.

Now I was beginning to get a little down. I wondered if all this was worth it. In my mind there was a terrible conflict. I would never be satisfied until I had traveled overland to India. But I didn't want to end my 1978 vacation with six weeks of hell and then spend a fortune to fly back to Europe to go home.

We walked around for the rest of the day checking out the glittering vault of royal jewels in the basement of Iran's biggest bank, and wandering around not too happy about our situation. It must have been close to 100 degrees. I kept trying to call my Persian friend from my dorm at the UW, Abdi. But I could never communicate with whoever answered. Finally, I got an Iranian to call and find that Abdi was vacationing at the Caspian Sea.

Amir Kabir is the cheapo hotel district where you're bound to run into anyone heading down the Hippie Trail to India. Hidden behind piles of tires and greasy auto parts are gross little hotels. We bumped into many people from our bus ride and found a terrible hotel for 400 rial, or $6. I think it was the worst ever for me, but I have a hunch I'm just getting more sensitive to filth, bugs, broken windows, and cigarette butts stuck in sooty holes in the hotel walls lit by bare-dangling bulbs. There we sat. As I pinched strange tiny bugs landing on my leg, my spirits sunk to a low point for this trip. I felt like a filthy animal and I thought of the easy life in Greece and Europe. Gene and I discussed the situation and he was strong and pepped up my spirits. I worried that maybe the whole thing was too rushed and maybe we should not do so much. I think that was a weakness in me aggravated by the lousy day and pathetic hotel we had here.

We went out for a soak in a public bath, but I got in an argument with the guy who was already charging us double the Iranian price and wanted to charge even more for soap. Of course, I'm rich compared to him and I'd hardly notice the gouge. But it was a matter of principle and I walked out. We bought a street-side dinner of cucumber, boiled eggs, and a hot potato with Cokes and enjoyed it back in our room. I took a sponge bath which raised me one step above the animal level. I was becoming like the other cheap, hip, road-to-India travelers who lived in their rooms like quiet animals in caves running around in sweaty underpants and bare feet that didn't care.

Sweltering under a sheet but more protected from bugs, a real bed felt good. I had no trouble finding sleep.

Tuesday, July 25: Tehran

Screeching buses and screaming boys woke us at 4:30 and broken sleep was the best I could get for the next couple hours. We checked out of our hole-tel, not trusting it enough to leave our bags there and we went down to the hip travelers' center of Tehran—a big cheap hotel called Amir Kabir—to get a room for tonight. We were wait-listed but left our packs in case a room opened up. And then, somehow, we managed to get tickets on the Thursday morning bus to Mashhad. That was a good feeling but now we had two days to hang around Tehran.

We picked up our Afghanistan visas and celebrated with the last of Sveti's mom's great cake and very good, clean, cold homogenized and pasteurized chocolate milk. A yummy treat.

We had pulled ourselves out of our confused state by buying a map of Tehran and now this huge city made some sense. We saw we were near the Pakistan embassy so headed off to get that visa as well.

We never found the embassy but that really didn't matter—we hit the jackpot by meeting a wonderful guy named Abbas—or "Abe to Americans."

He stopped to help us with our map. It's difficult when each new mayor decides to change all the street names. When he found out we were Americans he said, "Hey, come have a cup of coffee with me." He was so innocent and happy sounding that we couldn't turn him down. What a lucky break.

Abe apologized for his messy flat as he fixed us a sandwich, fruit, and a cold beer. He had a gorgeous little apartment and a lifestyle that was royal compared to the common masses filling the streets like we saw in Amir Kabir. Abe learned English from an American family, picked up Spanish because of his fanatical love for Spanish music, and put everything together to get a job for the government heading a translating department. When he was refused a raise, he was allowed to work parttime for whole pay. Continuing that game masterfully, he's now making good money and working about an hour a day!

Abe is quite a playboy. His dates are usually in the afternoon because Iranian girls are watched very closely by their parents, and they rarely live anywhere but at home until they are married. That doesn't stop very much with Abe though. His girlfriend was dreamy and very sexy. She stayed for a spaghetti dinner but had to head home for her 8:00 curfew.

Now Abe and Gene took turns playing his guitar—Abe Spanish and Gene pop. Abe just loved the way Gene and I sang old rock songs. We really had to pick our brains to keep coming up with singable tunes that we knew the words to.

We sat on his warm, starlit balcony eating ice cream and enjoying each other's music. I really was shocked at how good life can be for some and how relatively miserable it can be for others. This was a very rosy picture of Tehran—not a very comfortable city. (I had never cared about, or even noticed, what I was now realizing was a big ethical issue: the giant difference between rich people and poor people. Not between rich and poor countries...but the difference within countries.)

I loved my trusty Pentax K1000. We traveled with 36-shot rolls of film in cannisters and, packing light, we had a strict daily ration of shots so we didn't run out before the trip was over.

Later on, we watched Iranian TV. Iran is so geared to the USA that they have an American channel and radio station designed to broadcast the local stations in English. Abe and his friends just love to sit around and watch such classics as Rawhide, Top Cat, and Bob Newhart. The strange thing is, there are no commercials! I never realized what a valuable function commercials fulfilled. I need to break every now and then to rest, talk, or take a quick pee. Iranian TV is intense. It never lets up.

We watched the English news which seems to be more of a daily reminder that instability reigns all over this corner of the earth. You can't put a price tag on the value of being an American. I really wouldn't want it any other way. I'm spoiled.

Abe, Gene, and I had a great discussion about politics and economics relative to distinct cultures. Abe's obviously in a very good spot in Iranian society. He supported the Shah, saying idealistic, anti-Shah college students are well-meaning. But they don't realize that most people just couldn't handle all the freedoms that Americans have if they were just given to them overnight. The Shah did an experiment. He gave Tabriz total freedom and, apparently, they nearly tore the city apart. The Shah had to step in and enforce his kind of order.

Gene and I bedded down in Abe's living room and were happy not to be back in Amir Kabir.

Wednesday, July 26: Tehran

Gene got sick during the night. I don't know what hit him, but something sure did. We had a restful morning and then decided to brave the big bazaar.

Abe told us that the most expensive taxi fare in town was 50 rials. We had been paying 100-150 rials. That was the end of that. It's so nice to know the going rate. With that knowledge, we taxied cheap (less than 50 cents) down to the bazaar. Gene wasn't right and he decided to rest in a park for a few hours while I explored the thriving scene.

I walked and walked, enjoying plenty of encounters. To survive the barrage an American tourist with a fancy camera and short pants receives, you have to build a hard shell around you. You can step out and make fun things happen, but when things get too heavy, you must be able to pull back inside and mentally repel the onslaught—the grabbing hands, mothers holding babies while they crap in a corner, "Hello Misters," and the heat, dust, and puddles of muck that only beggars can ignore. It's kind of like putting your head under water—you can do it, but only for so long.

I surfaced and Gene felt worse. He decided to take a cab back to Abe's. I was glad he had a place to go. What an opportune time to have such a good local friend.

Now I was on my own and I had lots of things to do. First, I walked over to check out the big mosque that Abe recommended. The mosque is like a cool refuge for any Muslim to come and take a break from the hubbub of life on the street for a little while. While locals came here for an escape, I felt quite out of place. I felt like I came from a different planet.

I spent a few hours just wandering. The whole city was an experience. I was looking for postcards and there are very few in Tehran. I also needed something to make my stomach feel good, take care of my thirst, and give me energy. A hard-boiled egg and a 7-Up did the trick. Dirt abounds in Tehran and to eat food and nothing else is quite a trick.

Now it was 3:00 and the museum was opening. Flocking in, lost in a group of German tourists, I met a nice British girl who was flying home tonight. I felt a little envy. England sounds so cool, refreshing, enjoyable, and easy right now. For some reason, I am putting myself through this ordeal and I want to accomplish it. If I don't make it to India, I'll never be content. It will always bug me, and I'll probably end up on this same road on some later "vacation."

We enjoyed the museum together although there wasn't much of note to see. We enjoyed a cup of tea afterwards and said goodbye. Nice girl—I'd love to go to England.

No good tourist would leave Tehran without seeing its trademark—the Shah's Shahyad monument.

I took a long bus ride out to where the city meets the vast burnt wasteland and there, shining white over well-watered green lawns and fountains, stood the monument—like a squashed or very stunted Eiffel Tower. I was impressed and glad I made the trip out to see it.

Underneath was a dull museum and a great media show making Iran look much better than could ever be possible in real life. How awesome its mountains, how noble its cities, and how splendid the nearly deified Shah all were.

Too lazy to climb to the top, I walked around, enjoying the monument and then, after running through the sprinklers like a little kid, I caught a ride back downtown. It's so easy to get a taxi or even a private car to give you a ride. If you just point to the pavement in front of you, random cars will stop and let you hope in. Sometimes they charge; if you can make a friend by the end of the ride, you probably got there for free.

I was back at Abe's by 7:00. Gene was feeling pretty rough. He had slept most of the day and still wasn't better. Several friends had dropped by—Abe's place seemed to be the fun place to be. We watched a little TV and then I diligently made myself stamp and address my 25 postcards and start writing all those "obligatories." (With each trip I commit myself to writing these special people in my life and now seemed to be a good time to get that yearly task out of the way.)

Again, I was impressed by how Iranians gobble up American culture. Bob Newhart was great to see as was Rawhide. The shows go very quickly without commercials.

Faddi, Abe's sister, came by and everyone else left. Gene was sleeping in the living room and Abe asked him if he wanted a pizza. That seemed like a silly question to a guy who was really sick. Gene had an omelet while Abe ran out and picked up three Iranian pizzas. Italy is a very long way away.

Abe taught me some fancy backgammon strategies, beating me three times very quickly and then we checked on Gene. He had a fever and was quite down. We went to the pharmacy and for a minute it was thought that he might have cholera, which broke out in Turkey, but Gene's shots were up to date. We gave him some pill to break the fever and then all went to bed—waiting till morning to decide if we would stay put or go on to Mashhad. I fell asleep worrying about Gene and wishing I could do something to help but also thinking how I would restructure the trip if we turned back, and scolding myself for not really wanting to push on. Actually, I wanted to go both ways equally bad but for different reasons.

Thursday, July 27: Tehran to Mashhad, Iran

We were up at 5:00 and Gene felt better. Packing quickly, we had cake and coffee and Abe drove us down to the bus station. Doing his best to entice us to return someday soon, Abe bid us goodbye saying, "Americans just blast their heads off when they see the Iranian ski slopes!" Goodbye dear friend and giver of fun and comfort.

We met our Spanish friends from the Istanbul-Tehran trip and boarded the bus ready for the long day's ride to Mashhad.

At 6:00, we pulled out: about 40 Muslim pilgrims going to their holy place and us five tourists who were just curious enough to sit on this bus all day. The first six hours went by quickly. The bus was quiet, friendly, and orderly. The

This bus ride came with a wonderful little friend.

driver was safe and steady, stopping only rarely, and the scenery was dramatic. We passed through a high rugged mountain pass right next to the highest mountains in western Asia.

The Spaniards played the Rolling Stones on their tape recorder, we read, enjoyed the scenery, and I made friends with a gorgeous little Persian girl in front of me. I took some pictures of her that may be prize winners.

After 12:00, we came out of the mountains and into a hot, humid, sticky plain that just went on and on. The dust-caked, one-story towns all looked the same and served only to slow down traffic. The seats didn't recline and the plastic seat cover was quite yucky in the muggy heat. I felt like I had two knees in my kidneys but that's just the way some jerk designed the seats. My knees hate to spend the long day pressed tightly up against the too-close next seat, but they do it without so much as a whimper. The time dragged on.

Thankfully the bus, while slow, was very steady and we were happy just to make it in one day. We spent a lot of time looking at our Asia map and proving to ourselves that we've gone a very long way and we're nearly there now. The former may be true, but not the latter.

After a dinner stop where Gene had a chelo kebab, and I finally ate my can of ravioli that I bought in Frankfurt and carried all the way here, I realized this was the third Italian dinner in a row I'd had. Spaghetti, pizza, and now—saving the best for last—my delicious cold ravioli out of a can.

The last two hours dragged terribly until Gene started teaching me how to pick out the chords to songs without the music. That particular musical skill is my weakness and I wish so much that it could be my strength.

We got into Mashhad at midnight and it soon became apparent that there was not a room in town to be had. This was a very special holy time, and every Muslim and his brother was here. People were camped out on the roadsides for miles.

After failing to find a park that the police would let us sleep in, a friendly guy came to our rescue and got us a cab to take us to the Mashhad campground.

This place was great—complete with showers, a swimming pool, and soft grass to sleep on. All the tents and rooms were taken but for 100 rials, there was plenty of grass to sleep on.

Our Spanish friends—better prepared, set out their sleeping bags and tent while Gene and I (who had no tent or sleeping bags) put on our warm clothes and slept on our ponchos. I was so tired, I really wanted to sleep and I did.

Friday, July 28: Mashhad

I slept until the warm sun nudged me at 8:00 a.m. Our Spanish friends found that there was no bus to Afghanistan until tomorrow. We almost begged a ride from three German VW vans but they said there wasn't room (there was lots). So, we just would spend the day in Mashhad and get an early start in the morning.

This was a holy city at a holy time and it was full of people trying to be holy at the holy shrine. We were hustled from the time we left the campsite. It was kind of strange. The campsite was for tourists only and local Iranians would gather around the fences and peer in. It was nice to have such a refuge.

A guy drove us to the bus station, waited while we bought a ticket to the Afghan border, and took us downtown near the shrine. We went up with him

Top: In Iran, the last Shah was still in power, but just barely. His portraits, which permeated society, seemed ready to crash to the ground. Bottom: Visiting the Mashad Holy Shrine; young men build brooms in the local bazaar.

for awful tea and his motives became clear. He wanted to sell us rugs and turquoise. We excused ourselves and made our way to the shrine.

The holy shrine was gorgeous with its turquoise dome gleaming in the hot blue sky. Pilgrims all flocked there and we were the only non-Muslims. There was always some guy following us telling us not to go closer and come to his shop. We worked our way right up to the elaborate gates and then could look in where Christians cannot go.

Just hanging around, we had an interesting time mingling and gawking. After a cooling down hose off, we ventured into the bazaar, shared a melon, checked out an old mosque, shook an overly friendly clinger, and walked down a long, quiet street in search of food. That's a very formidable task in Mashhad. I bought a liter of milk which turned out to be something else in a milk carton, and we stumbled into a bread shop and studied their interesting mass production of flat breads cooked as if slapping small pizza crusts onto the wall of a hot underground oven.

Friendly Iranians gathered to see what was up with the vagabond Yankees who had just dropped in.

I was tired and Gene felt sick, so we caught a ride back to the campground and sacked out. Later we went for a refreshing swim, baked in the fierce sun, and wrote in our journals. We got a tent with a real bed tonight for 150 rials instead of 100 for a piece of the grass. That was much better.

I sat by the pool writing and then went out to try and buy some dinner. Many things added up to really bring me down on this place. I wanted some French cheese but the guy in the store was obviously ripping me off. A lady before me was just sold the same thing for about half the price. I walked on through the filthy, dusty streets in my protective shell ignoring the faceless little "Hello Misters" and not finding anything but apples and milk that I knew how to eat.

Back in the campground, Gene and I were talking about diarrhea, which he had and I didn't. I commented that I had had no problems in eight weeks of travel this summer. I shouldn't have said that because a few minutes later I heard it knocking and ran off to the toilet.

We went up to the restaurant and shared a bowl of lemony soup with bread and our treated water. We have passed the edge of safe water and from now on it's iodine or halazone tablets. We must have looked funny—two grown men sharing a meager bowl of soup. It didn't hit the spot.

We went to bed early knowing we had to be up at 6:00 without any alarm clock to catch our bus to Afghanistan in the morning. Our beds were fine. I ushered out a giant green grasshopper-type bug and we slept fine.

Saturday, July 29   Meshad – Herat

My Spanish friend woke me at 5:45. I think ~~would have slept~~ _____ _____ if he hadn't ____ ____ ____ ____ down to ____ stati ____ ____ ____ ____ for breakfas ____ ____ ____ way. did qu ____ ____ world.
Here w ____ ____ compared to Afqanis loo ____ ____ iranians + Afqanis _____ bundles filled the bus station. Our bus left at 7:20 and was pretty full of western travellers – the most we had seen since the Istanbul – Teheran bus.
Gene + I were quiet + weak. I kind of sat there, hot wind blowing in my face with my hair whipping around, hoping the kilometers would tick by ____ ____ ____ I was plunging farther + fast ____ ____ ____ ____

CHAPTER 4
Good Stuff—Afghanistan
July 29–August 3

Saturday, July 29:
Mashhad to Herat, Afghanistan

My Spanish friend woke me at 5:45. I think I would have slept all morning if he hadn't come in. We caught a ride down to the station and, weakly, I searched for breakfast. Half a liter of milk and a small cake did quite nicely and we were on our way.

Here was the beginning of a new world. Afghanis look Asian and Mongolian compared to Iranians, and Afghanis and their twine-wrapped bundles of belongings filled the bus station. Our bus left at 7:20 and was pretty full of Western travelers—the most we had seen since the Istanbul-Tehran bus.

Gene and I were quiet and weak. I just sat there—not moving or talking, hot wind blowing in my face with my hair whipping around, hoping the kilometers would tick by, and knowing I was plunging farther and farther away from Europe.

At 10:30 we came to the desolate Iran-Afghanistan border. What a place! Just stuck in the middle of nowhere. We gave up our passports and walked into the building. An interesting museum with a message greeted us. In several glass cases shared the stories and hiding places of many ill-fated drug smugglers. It made for interesting reading—who smuggled what in, how they were caught, and where they are doing time in prison. I have this terrible fear that someone will plant some dope in my rucksack and I'll get framed. That would be no fun at all…in fact, end of vacation.

We got through the Iranian customs rather easily and then we walked across a windy desert no man's land to a place bordered by abandoned, disassembled

Welcome to sunny Afghanistan

The Iran-Afghanistan border was a god-forsaken place where customs officials, police, and con artists seemed to outnumber travelers. From there, we negotiated a bus ride to the first city in Afghanistan, Herat.

VW vans and full of local people piling into small orange buses. We just stood around. The wind and heat were fierce. The barren plain stretched out in every direction and I said to Gene, "So this is Afghanistan." We found shade in one of the wrecked VW vans and peeled a small apple. Then a bus came and we piled in. Stopping for a quick passport check, I couldn't believe it was so easy. It wasn't.

A few minutes later our bus pulled into the search yard and we unloaded to sit and wait for the bank and doctor's office to open up.

And here I sit. The time is good for nothing but catching up in the journal, which I finally did, and thinking. As I flick and brush big ants off me and shield my eyes from sand and blowing things, I fantasize about all the fun things I could be doing. (It also occurs to me how, when you're right up to date, journal writing can be more vivid…how you can do a better job.) I think of friends back home, of my parents at leisure in their boat up in cool, green, refreshing British Columbia and the fun I could be having in Europe. I am glad I'm finally doing this but I'm really looking forward to the end of it all. I'm hoping for health, no hassles, and a good flight back to Europe.

The funny little bank opened up and to change my 100-francs note I had to make three signatures, write down the serial number of the bill, and ask several times for the correct change. I came away with 775 afghanis.

The next few hours tried my patience as we bounced from one dusty office to the next getting everything taken care of so we could enter Afghanistan. Gene was missing a shot on his yellow International Certificate of Vaccination (which we show at each border) so we were sent to the little clinic. There we waited and waited until the doctor dropped by. I will never forget the sight of his dull needle bending as he forced it into Gene's arm for that shot. With our shot certificate now complete, we shuffled further through the border crossing process. The luggage "search" was little more than a glance, our shot certificates were checked again, the police and the customs officers checked us out, we had Fanta, and then finally everyone packed back onto the orange bus and we were on our way—or so we thought.

About 100 yards later there was a police check and most of the Polish travelers on the bus flunked it and had to go through more red tape. Then we headed into the dusty vastness of the Afghanistan wasteland.

The countryside was dry and barren, backed by stark brown mountains, and broken every once in a while by a cluster of mud huts, some old ruins, or a herd of goats or sheep. It always feels good to enter a new country. So far this summer I've only explored two new ones. But everything that lies ahead is as new as can be.

Afghanistan, here we come!

Just when it looked like we were getting somewhere, a dispute broke out in the front of the bus. The Afghanis decided to double the price of the ride from 50 to 100 afghani. Why not? Us tourists were stubborn and we refused. One rugged looking Afghan pulled a knife while the driver turned around and threatened to take us back to the Iranian border. You could say they had us over a barrel.

There was an uproar as everyone was trying to solve the problem at once. One soft-spoken but commanding Pakistani urged us to pay but we all believed if we paid there was nothing stopping them from pulling the same trick again. We compromised—giving them 60 afghanis now and paying the rest upon arrival in Herat. After that episode we were all on edge, and I think if they tried to get any more money, they would have had a lot of trouble from their worldly bus load of hardened travelers.

Rest stop entertainment? A goat being skinned.

We stopped at a desolate tea shop with a well and a bunch of locals skinning a still-warm goat. There was a sign reading "hotel," and I expected the worst. Lots of people are notorious for "highly recommending" certain hotels. But this was just an innocent tea stop, and it provided Gene and me with our first good look at Afghanistan. The leaky well provided everyone with cold, filthy water. I wallowed in it, really cooling down nicely. We shared a 25-cent melon and my weak, starving body gobbled it down. I feel like I've really abused myself by not eating much. For two days I've forgone any real meals and just drank pop and sucked on melons. Gene and I decided from now on to raise our standard of living: We'd eat well and stay in good hotels for both our mental and physical health and to keep our spirits high.

The tea house was exactly the image I had for an Afghanistan tea house. Old traditionally clad men, who looked like they worked hard but who never seem to do anything but lazily sit around, sitting on threadbare rugs on the floor drinking tea and smoking hashish. The room filled with smoke and their glassy dark eyes smiled. A few of us tourists joined them, but I just stood over my melon rinds looking in the window like I was watching a documentary on TV. The word spread—our driver was high and the crew would be quite mellowed out. What a bizarre society. I guess when materially you're so far behind you just give up—sit in the shade eating melons, drinking tea, and smoking hash.

Back in the hot bus we made it to Herat and it dawned on us: "You know, this place looks quite nice." We were definitely in a new and different culture and both Gene and I perked up. I punched him on the shoulder and said, "Ok, now our trip begins!"

Herat was, like our minimal guidebook info said, "hard not to like." Very green as far as towns in this part of the world go and with lots of parks, I liked Herat right away. Sick of cheap, scuzzy holes, I lobbied for a first-class hotel. We found a dilly.

Hotel Mowafaq, the fanciest hotel in downtown Herat, was just what we needed. Centrally located, showers, swimming pool, clean restaurant, and free of all the con men who plague cheaper hotels, this would lift our spirits mightily. I feel like a bit of a softy, but I love a place that I can leave my stuff in without worrying, walk around in bare feet, and get easy peace when I need it. Our double cost only 200 afghanis ($5) and we were prepared to spend more.

We had a Sprite and walked around this central square of Herat, stopping in a small clothing shop where Gene and I might get some local clothes so we can go "native" for the rest of the trip. The local baggy clothes make a lot more sense and they'd be fun souvenirs too. Gene ended up buying a chunk of hashish for about $1

A few extra dollars provided a quiet oasis.

from the guy. Getting high for my first time was on my list of desired experiences for this trip. We'll wait and see what we'll do with it.

Now we were ready to clean up and have a feast. A lovely cold shower and an enjoyable and highly successful stint on the real sit-down toilet (you don't appreciate life's little things—like a toilet to sit on—until you don't have them). Stepping out of the bathroom I thought, "Nice, the diarrhea I had yesterday was just a quick little punishment for bragging how I'd been traveling with solid stools for two months, and now I am a new man…back to normal."

This man wanted to show off his fine turban…and he did.

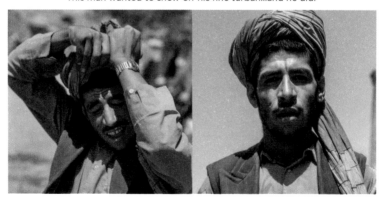

What did the people think as we waltzed in and out of their lives?

Downstairs we ordered the two local specialties that they served on Saturdays, and we noticed that the menu had a little note on each page. Since the People's Revolution, all prices are lowered by 10 afghanis. That made each meal cost only 50 afghanis ($1.25) for soup, bread, rice, meat, and cold water. We were both thirsty and the cold water attacked our self-discipline like the forbidden fruit. We succumbed to it and it was good. I couldn't help feeling "iffy" about it, like I always do when I drink questionable water, but that didn't cut down on its initial goodness. Black and green tea in good sized pots finished the meal nicely and I can't believe how everything about this trip has turned around so wonderfully.

The people here are welcoming, and soldiers and police are present on the streets in the wake of the recent revolution. Horse-drawn, chariot-like, flower-decorated taxis charge down the streets. We stood on our breezy balcony under the stars, overlooking the city, and thinking the only thing not different about this place is the constellations.

My hair is fluffy, there's air conditioning in the hall, and a bug screen on our open window. Rather than dangling homeless, the light has a fixture. My teeth are clean, my stomach is full, I feel healthy (and hopefully expect to be tomorrow), and I think I'll go to bed early tonight. It's so important to live good and enjoy oneself. And, without going through periods of misery and discomfort, you can't really know what it is to enjoy. I am getting better at enjoyment. I'm becoming more appreciative.

Sunday, July 30: Herat

A dream woke me at 7:30 and by 8:15 I gave up trying to fall back to sleep. Down at the restaurant I enjoyed two fried eggs, yogurt, and a pot of black chai. After cleaning my camera lenses, Gene and I set out to see Herat.

First, we had two pieces of business: change money and get bus tickets. The bank was really something. It took nearly an hour to change my $100, but just sitting there watching the Afghani banking process was interesting. I saw suitcases of tattered afghanis, tribesmen coming in with five or six $100 bills (I'm afraid to imagine where they got them), a uniformed guard with a bayonet long enough to skewer five or six bank robbers, and a rag-tag building and atmosphere. I had 3,858 afghanis coming to me. First the guy gave me 3,000. I said "more," and he gave me 800. "More" and I got 50 more afghanis and then I asked for and got the last 8 afghanis.

Next, Gene and I booked a bus ride to Kabul on the highly recommended Qaderi bus company. The 800-kilometer ride cost only $5, or 200 afghanis. Hopefully, we will get our seats and there will be no hanky-panky.

We were free to ramble. I had a Fanta, put on my zoom lens, and went into action on a dreamy side street full of colorful flowery horse-drawn taxis, busy craftsmen, fruit stands, and dust. Each man who passed looked like something straight out of a travel poster. Strong powerful eyes behind leathery weather-beaten faces. Poetic wind-blown beards long and scraggily and turbans like snakes wrapping protectively around their heads. Old women totally covered by bag-like outfits carried children and called out, strangely enough, for photos.

We wandered away from the main center coming to a dusty residential area churning with activity. I didn't really know how people accepted us strange short-panted, pale-skinned, weak-stomached, finnicky people who came into their world to gawk, take pictures, and buy junk to bring home and tell everyone how cheap it was. I couldn't help but feel like us curious tourists got old to these hardy, proud people who work so hard and live so simply.

There were countless moments and scenes that blazed forever in my mind, a picture of Afghanistan. We worked up a mean thirst and we shared a watermelon in the shade before moving on.

A bit tired, we headed back to our lovely hotel, had a plate of potatoes, a bowl of soup, and some chai and went up for a shower and a short snooze. We are really living well now for a change. I cashed that $100 and it feels so good to just spend money when you want to and not worry.

Now we went back into the sun. The afternoon temperature was still cooking and every once in a while we'd soak our heads under a faucet. After mailing our postcards, we checked out a row of the cloth weavers. Hard-working men ran these ingeniously primitive looms tirelessly. Quite interesting to witness. Then, making a wide circle, we came to the big mosque, checked it out, and found ourselves in a neighborhood of very hard-sell shops.

One pseudo-friendly guy took me by the hand and walked me into his shop and before I knew it, I was wearing the wonderful white baggy pants and shirt and turban of the local people and bargaining madly. I was determined to work him down from 500 to my ceiling of 152 afghanis. I almost made it, but I was surprised when he let me walk away empty handed, a bit sad too. I want those cool, baggy, low-profile clothes and maybe, if I can swallow my pride, I'll go back tomorrow and get them.

Like running the gauntlet, we made our way in and out of shops back to our hotel. I tried and failed to get a lovely mink skin cheap. I did offer 200 afghanis for an exciting Afghan fox hat and ended up buying it and I proudly worked a guy down from 600 afghanis to 100 each for three little nicely embroidered pouches. I haven't bought any souvenirs to speak of in two months of travel—now I'm afraid I've opened the floodgates.

Back at the hotel, Gene pulled out the hunk of hashish that he bought and this, I decided, would be the time and place that'd I'd lose my "marijuana virginity." I've never even smoked a cigarette and smoking pot has always turned me off, so to speak, because it's always an object of social pressure, and I would never feel comfortable doing it because everyone at a party was doing it and I

Ready to take "going local" to new heights, I stopped by a tailor, got measured, and purchased a made-to-order, all-white outfit.

Afghanistan towns invited exploration.

was the only "square" one. That kind of pressure and the usual scene surrounding pot smoking reinforced my determination to stay away from the evil weed. But this—being here in Afghanistan—made things different.

In Afghanistan, hashish is an integral part of the culture. It's as innocent as wine with dinner is in America. If ever I was to experience this high, it wouldn't be in a dark dorm room at the UW with a bunch of people I didn't respect. I could never feel good about that.

Gene and I talked about marijuana and hash for about three hours on the bus after we left Istanbul. I decided that, if I felt good about the whole situation, I'd like to smoke some hash in Afghanistan. Well, here I am in Herat, I feel great, and I love this town. We got about half a domino worth of pure hashish for 40 afghanis ($1). It was so smooth it had to be sliced with a knife.

Up in the room, Gene mixed it with some tobacco and piled the product into a funny, old, straight wood pipe we picked up. He took a drag—immediately remarking, "Good stuff." I sucked in, not knowing what to expect and hoping not to get a mouth full of ashes. I don't like smoke, but besides that, there was nothing repulsive about it. It didn't even smell bad like marijuana. The only problem was nothing happened. I had smoked enough but virgin runs are generally unproductive. It felt good anyway—I had done it.

We went out for a walk. Going from shop to shop very casually. Mixing with people, nosing into shops, and just poking around. This place is small but it really doesn't matter because no street is ever the same if you walk through it a second or third time.

For dinner, we sat outside of our restaurant since there was a special wedding tonight in the big room. We had a plate of lots of different vegetables with lots of meat washed down by tea for $1.50 each.

Upstairs we smoked a bit more and took a cold shower. This time I sensed a bit of a change. Certain colors and objects were more tangy. Things had a vibrant edge that I didn't realize was an option. I was very relaxed and the light fixture on our ceiling looked like a big candle breathing in and out. But I still wasn't really high. Or, maybe I was…

Downstairs the big wedding had begun and the bride's father proudly shook my hand welcoming Gene and me, and we sat next to the little Afghan band listening to the exciting music and watching the women dance. Everyone was quite formal, the men were in one room, the women in the other, and the decorated car waited parked outside.

Now we took a nighttime walk. Chariots with torches charged through the darkness, men carried lanterns, shopkeepers and the work boys squatted around soup and bread, many Afghans were high or getting there, it was cool and, like always, the wind howled. The night was a great experience and we wandered.

After a small melon, checking out the wedding once more, taking a cold shower with our sheets and making a nice wet bed, we commented on what a good day today was and, looking forward to tomorrow and wrapped in wet sheets, we went to sleep.

Monday, July 31: Herat

I didn't stir for nine hours. After breakfast we picked up our rental bikes and began a little adventure. It felt good to have wheels. We could stop when we wanted and, if the people got too intense, we could make a clean escape. The breeze cooled us off and things happened at a much faster rate than when we traveled on foot.

Speeding through the part of town we already knew well, we headed for the old, ruined minarets that we saw when we approached Herat two days ago. Checking out this historic site, an old man let us in the mosque for 10 afghanis and we saw the tomb of an old Afghan king.

Now we had seen the big historic site and we stopped to visit with some studious types in the shade. We had a nice chat and learned something about the culture and language. (It seems that educated people around the world are likely to speak English.) We also learned from our friend that we were spending too much money for just about everything.

Coasting happily down the road, we were surrounded by Herat: guys tossing melons, colorful girls sitting on curbs, lazy teenagers slouching on warm

Left: Trucks were exuberantly painted, though many vehicles in Afghanistan are still horse-drawn. Right: I felt like we were bringing smiles from distant lands to children who were confused, curious, and happy to see us.

wagons, and lots of little tidbits of Afghan life. The people are genuinely friendly and proud, shaking my hand firmly and as equals. While I did get one small fruit thrown at me, all in all, this is one of the friendliest countries I've experienced. Of course, it's a different world for women. Any woman (and post-pubescent girl) who ventures onto the streets is totally covered up, seeing only through a tiny gridwork in the cloth that covers her face.

We were determined to pedal in one direction until we reached the edge of town. After wetting our whistles with a Sprite, we made our way down the busy, dusty street until the city became more of a mud village like ones I'd seen in Egypt and Morocco. Taking side roads, we found ourselves enveloped in a new and different world. Quiet, brown mud streets became high walls long and narrow. The walls were broken occasionally by small shops and rustic wooden doors. Young and old sat around as if they were waiting for a stranger on a bike to happen by. I'm sure we were a very rare sight for them. I wonder if they enjoyed our presence or if we were violating their peace.

I experimented with different greetings, from a salute to a child's wave, to the solemn "kiss the hand and put it to the heart" that religious-looking types

Hey, can I help you thrash your wheat?

offer us. That one gets great results. I had a pocket full of candies for gifts and I feel better giving that than giving money.

You know, everyone in this happy society seems content and I've seen no hunger and very few hard-case beggars. They have modest needs for their meager productivity and things seem to work out just fine, and there's more than enough tea, hashish, and melons for everyone.

We poked around until we had had our fill and realized that this was hot and hard work. Then, on the way back, we stopped off at a pile of hay being romantically thrashed by a couple of oxen pulling a wooden hay-chewing device. What a dreamy tourist opportunity! I pounced on the chance to drive the cart and had an unforgettable blast. I got to sit on the chewer, driving the oxen around and around, and I think the peasants got as big of a kick out of me as I got out of them and their hay. That's optimality.

We got our bikes back after two hours and paid a buck each. We picked up a melon and retreated to our hotel. Feeling hot but happy, we stopped off at the pool, stripped to our underwear and took the chilly plunge. Instant refreshment! Wow! What a fantastic day we're having! We frolicked around, took a few dives, relaxed in the sun and I thought, "My goodness—this is what a vacation is supposed to be." Dripping up to the room, we sacked out for a while and went down for lunch. Good sleep, good food, and a good hotel—that was my formula for the rest of this trip to be enjoyable and successful.

After a rest and a few cold showers, the sun was a bit lower in the sky and we stepped back out. While I was deep into a bargaining match with a nice guy for the mink I had fallen in love with, Martin from the Istanbul-Tehran bus dropped by. We chatted and he highly recommended the "endless bazaar." We said we were heading there.

I had my zoom lens on and I got such a thrill out of zooming in on these lovely people. I can hardly wait to see my pictures. (It's a shame there's no way to see and review what kind of pictures you're getting on the road until after you return home.) We morphed or melted from scene to scene soaking in all the bazaar images. What a sensual experience. We'd pass from water-pipe-making souks, to tin pounders, weavers, beadmakers, bead stringers, people working billows, people sharpening knives on rickety foot-powered wheels, chain pounders, and nail benders. Everything was hand-done. Old and young worked furiously at the same menial task all day long—all lifelong. I'll never again complain about a long day of my work—teaching piano lessons.

Each shop was about five yards across, and every five yards was a new scene—a new glimpse of Afghan life. Some things we couldn't even understand. At one point, little children wouldn't give up asking for "baksheesh" (gifts of money) and we had to duck into a huge mosque where a policeman chased them away.

Now we were exhausted. Back at the hotel we went for a swim and a strange dog knocked my glasses off my bag and the lens fell out. I was worried but it popped back in—apparently good as new. I dread the thought of breaking my glasses and having to wear my high school hornrims that I brought for a spare.

Up in the room we tried out a little more hash and went out to mingle. Mingling was a bit intensified. Little things, like a man weighing tomatoes, tickled me special and I was more receptive to would-be pests and ready to poke around a little more freely. I didn't know if it was because of the hashish or because I was in a very good mood.

We hopped in a funny little three-wheeled taxi, that looked like a souped-up ice cream truck, for a ride to another part of town and I really got into some exciting photography. Existing light and lantern light subjects. I got men to pose precisely how I like them. I would even shove their chin up a tad or move the lantern closer. They could be exceptional or they might not, but both my subject and I had a memorable time trying.

We goofed around some more and then hopped on a fancy two-wheeled, horse-drawn buggy taxi. Charging all over town as if in a chariot, we sang songs—really entertaining, or at least amusing, our driver. We surprised him with a confident 10 afghanis and he barely had time to gripe as we hopped off. These tourists weren't taken for a ride except on a horse. I decided that if you try to agree to a price before boarding, they know you're new at the game and they'll rip you off. If you just get on and say, "Home James" and pay them what you think is reasonable, you'll do fine.

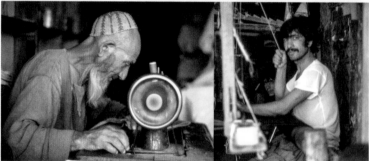

No museums, no turnstiles. Just stroll down the street, immersed in Afghanistan at work and at play. Every few meters, there was another shop with a hard-working businessman.

On our way home, I bought a lovely little five-afghanis (1 cent) goody. Then we stopped by to check out my friend with the mink skin. I knew I'd find myself bargaining furiously again and that's what happened. This was my third time in his shop and I knew if I went home without that mink, I'd kick myself. I love it just like I loved old "Ringworm" (a cat I befriended and took home back in second grade—that gave me ringworm). I finally went to 460 afghanis ($12) and came away with a great skin.

Now we were hungry and our hotel awaited. We are living so fantastically. Sitting down where the waiters know us, we ordered a hearty, meaty meal with tea and a melon. We've been drinking the water and my stools are solid so we had more of that. I feel so good. I'm in control, and anything I desire, I can just get it. Wow.

Up in the room, I took a long shower, cleaned up my pack, enjoyed my little souvenirs, and hit the sack. I laid there with nothing on wondering how cockroaches got their name. (Maybe I am high, after all.)

People enjoy the same things all over the world. The old cleaning man ignored my plea for more toilet paper and said dreamily, "Look, isn't it beautiful?" We both stood motionless on the roof of the hotel watching torch-toting chariots gallop by as the sun sank behind the distant mountain.

Earlier today, we were sitting and talking with some studious Afghans in a park when one asked, "Aren't you traveling with your women?" I said my girlfriend is at home and he replied, "Oh that's very difficult—I could never do that." I do feel like I've been "on the road" for a long time now.

Tuesday, August 1: Herat to Kabul

At 4:00, we were woken up and it was dead night. No one should be awake at that hour but there I sat on the edge of my bed. We had a melon and caught our 5:00 Qaderi bus to Kabul.

The bus was organized, punctual, and we were moving. Dawn was cracking as those sleeping on the sidewalks began to stir. Our boisterous bus honked loudly as if it was psyching itself up for the 800 kilometer ride that lay ahead. The road was good and we kept a steady speed, stopping only for a quick Coke all morning. The countryside was desolate, hot, and foreboding. A herd of camels, a stray nomad or cluster of quiet tents, a mud brick ruin melting like a sandcastle after being hit by a wave, and the solitary electricity line accompanied the narrow, but well-paved, US- and USSR-built road across the Afghanistan desert. It really was not a scenic ride, but I gained an appreciation for the vastness of this country of 10 million people by the time the 14-hour ride was over.

On a long bus ride, this mom and daughter stared at me, and I pondered the lot of women in this male-dominated world.

We had one short lunch stop where Gene and I had a Fanta and some peanuts, and then we raced on. This was the greatest ride. Our driver actually wanted to keep a good tempo. The countryside didn't change all day. The same lazy, goofy camels and sleepy gray-brown mudbrick castle towns kept passing with the stark dirt mountains providing a jaggy skyline.

Rest stops were fast: the men peed on one side of the road and the women, gathering on the other side, turned their black robes into one-person tents, and squatted with wrap-a-round privacy. Seeing a dozen short, round, black figures all squatting and still at the same time on the hard pan ground reminded me of some fantasy chess game. We also had three stops to pray to Mecca where everyone got out, kneeled, and bowed in the same direction. Being the only ones not partaking in the ritual left us feeling a bit awkward.

Then, just as darkness fell, we entered Kabul. Gene wasn't feeling well so we took a cab to touristy "Chicken Street" and found the nicest hotel we could— the not-too-nice, but ok, Sina Hotel.

Gene went straight to sleep while I had a lousy dinner with a friendly student from Philadelphia who was here to study the language. I'm spoiled after our great Herat hotel.

Oh well, I'm in Kabul. Imagine that. So close to my dream: the Khyber Pass and India. I do believe I'm more than halfway around the world from Seattle. I'll have to check a globe. I hope Gene's better—and I'm still good—in the morning.

Wednesday, August 2: Kabul

It's a mistake to go to bed without a watch. I slept ok but got up too early. Gene was in pretty sad shape so he stayed in bed. For breakfast I had a melon, a big carrot, and two boiled eggs and tea in the Sina Hotel courtyard. I was laid back from the start today because I knew we had two days in Kabul and there wasn't much to get excited about. I talked with a German girl who was just recovering from an eight-day bout with "Tehran tummy" and who wanted to go home. Home is a very nice thought when you're traveling to India. It's even more appealing when you're sick.

Getting down to business, I walked to the Pakistan bus company and got tickets for over the Khyber Pass into Pakistan for Friday morning. Then, with several incredibly persistent shoeshine boys tailing me, I ducked into the Pakistani embassy and was happy to learn that Americans need no visas to travel through Pakistan. We were set. Wow—Khyber Pass, Pakistan, and then on to India!

Back at the hotel, I checked on Gene. He was feeling very rugged still. I brought him special magic tea and two boiled eggs and hung around for a while. His tendency was to fast and sleep it off.

It was quite hot now as I set out to cover Kabul, what an unenviable task. I had no map or information. I really couldn't get oriented in this blobby, hodge-podge capital. The city is like a giant village sprawling out along several valleys. Where those valleys came together was downtown. Kabul seems to love its sadly dried-up river, which has very little water with a wide and rocky bed. It was hot and dusty, shade was rare, and I felt very obvious being white, alone,

and wearing shorts. Nevertheless, I walked and wandered, covering a good part of Kabul.

I walked through some very seedy parts, searched in vain for the tourist information place, and caught a taxi to the Kabul Museum. It was a long ride and he fiercely resisted the 40 afghanis I paid him. He wanted 60. I thought 40 was very fair and finally just to lose him I paid 50. Then I found out that the museum I came to see was closed. Feeling a bit frustrated and down on the people who heckled and gathered around me, I hopped onto a crowded bus and rode it to its end which was just where I wanted to be—generic, neighborhood Kabul. This was a busy place. The only real city in Afghanistan and it had quite a number of large buildings and fancy institutes. But the tribal chaos

Lots of men were in uniforms, but for some reason, it seemed tribal robes would be a better fit.

permeates everything. Around a modern department store there are old men with donkey loads of tomatoes, little girls selling small limes, piles of honeydew melons with a guy sitting on top sleepily smoking hash.

I checked out a fancy hotel and sat in the cool bar sipping a Coke and eating a nice girl's bread, and then I walked up to the top of "Afghan store," the closest thing to a Western department store, and found a nice restaurant with a beautiful view of ugly Kabul.

An old man had me sit with him and he said, "I am professor so and so. What is your name and fame?" He was very excited to have a meal with an American but I'm afraid I wasn't really in the proper mood and I wasn't very talkative. He told me he would never forget his meal with "Mr. Rick." I taught him the do-re-me scale and what a radish was. That was the only thing on my plate that stumped him in English.

Before he left, my professor friend told me, "A third of the people on this planet eat with spoons and forks like you, a third of the people eat with chopsticks, and a third of the people eat with their fingers like me…and we're all civilized just the same."

He left and I finished my meal under the silent stares of the other diners and then I headed home. As I walked, I thought that professor was right. I thought less of people like him who ate with their fingers. And I was wrong—ethnocentric. I was thankful for the lesson he taught me.

The evidence of the recent revolution is everywhere. Our bus was checked (for guns I assume) upon entering Kabul, copies of the headlines on the day of the change are seen posted, there's an 11:00 curfew, and soldiers are everywhere with poised bayonets. On the street I saw what was left of a tank, blown to bits and left as a reminder that the old regime was dead.

Later we ventured into our cozy little Sina Hotel courtyard for the mild dinner. I worked on a honeydew melon, we both had boiled eggs, and tea. Gene had some of Sina's special "sick man's tea." The rest of the evening was lazy and dull. I wasn't looking forward to another day in Kabul but there was no earlier bus and staying put another day would be better for Gene.

Thursday, August 3: Kabul

Today was malaria pill day and the end of our third week on the road. We were at the doorstep of India, most of our work was behind and most of the adventure was ahead. Our health was tenuous at best but both of us were determined that nothing would stop us now. I swallowed my super vitamin with zinc pills with black tea and had toast and eggs before going out for a

All across Asia, it was a man's world. If women were on the street, they were covered up.

walk. I had no big plans for today—just pass the time and enjoy myself.

I walked down "Chicken Street," the touristic high-pressure point of Afghanistan, oblivious to the countless "Come into my shop mister" invitations and realizing that out of all the junk everyone's trying to sell, there was nothing I really wanted.

I dropped by the American center to do a little reading and escape the noon sun, and later I got Gene to join me. That was about the first time he'd been out of the hotel in nearly two days. We just relaxed and read old news. The latest Time magazine was censored by the new government here. They censor any issue with articles about the USSR. (I don't understand the news, but the USSR seems hell-bent on getting messed up in Afghanistan and my hunch is that they're underestimating the spine of this poverty-stricken nation.) All the censorship left us only with old news to read. It's just not the same, but it's better than nothing. Reading American magazines on the road is like going to an American movie on the road—it brings you home for as long as you're immersed in it.

After laying around the hotel for a while, I put on Gene's baggy, white Afghan pants, grabbed my camera, and caught a bus to the edge of town. It's kind of nice not knowing or caring where you're going. I just got on any old bus, paid one afghani, and rode it for as long as I wanted—which was the end of the line. The bus driver invited me for tea, I accepted, and the gang gathered around to stare. Boy, I must really be a strange-looking dude to these people—they can stare endlessly. Last night I wrote a poem called "Afghan Eyes" about a little girl who stared at me for five hours on our bus ride from Herat.

Hopping back on a bus, I was soon back in the touristy world of "Chicken Street." Gene was tired of being cooped up and he finally had an appetite. I was having a little loose-bowel trouble myself and, after taking several alternate turns each on the toilet, we walked slowly down the street to find dinner.

The "Steak House" caught my eye when we first came to Kabul and now we would try it out. I wasn't counting on anything fantastic—just hoping. Actually, I got a very good steak-and-vegetable dinner for less than a dollar, complete with soup and a pot of tea. That hit both of our spots wonderfully. After the meal, we did a little money changing—trading our Iranian and Turkish money for Pakistani rupees.

(We kept hearing about unfortunate travelers who changed money in anticipation of a border crossing and ended up with money that had been taken out of circulation a few years earlier and was totally worthless. Paper money is generally filthy and extremely worn and it's really tough to know what's currently in circulation. With each time we change money, we're a bit nervous that we could be ripped off that way…but it never happened.)

We felt better after that good meal and went back home. I spent the evening in the courtyard catching up in this journal, repairing a strap on my pack, and enjoying tea and a Fleetwood Mac tape. It will be very good to be on the move again tomorrow.

Being so rich (even as a lowly backpacker) and so white in this poor and struggling corner of our world puts me in a strange bind as a traveler that I wish I could change. It's kind of sad, but I realized today that I tend to build a wall between me and any potential friends in this beyond-Europe part of the world. In Europe I love to talk with people and make friends. That's even a primary reason for my travels there, but here there's something in the way. I think a lot of it is suspicion, lack of understanding, and fatigue. Also, most of the people who I encounter around here who speak English, seem to speak it only to make money off the tourist. I wish I could totally trust people. And I wish I spoke the local language. But I can't and I don't.

Friday, Aug 4th   Kabul – Rawalpindi, Pakistan

This was the morning I was psyched for. I don't think I could have woken up feeling bad and I didn't _____ _____ good. We had a last _____ _____ caught our little _____

This b_____ _____ Khyber Pass. I h_____ _____ romantic wild & histo_____ _____ years and it was very _____ _____ list of thing to do – in the top five _____ sure. Now I was sitting on this kinky old brightly but badly painted bus next to a wonderful open window that let me lean half of my body out if I wanted to. Our seats were big & high yet crowded and the bus was full of Pakistan and the "Road to India" _____ _____ was glad to ge_____ _____ _____ we were _____ to the b_____ _____st standards _____ seen _____

CHAPTER 5

The World Opened Up—Over the Khyber Pass, Through Pakistan, and on to India

August 4–6

Friday, August 4:
Kabul to Rawalpindi, Pakistan

This was the morning I was psyched for. Both Gene and I felt good. We had a last big Sina Hotel breakfast and caught our little 8:30 bus to Pakistan.

This bus was the way I wanted to do Khyber Pass. I had dreamed of crossing this romantically wild and historically dangerous pass for years and it was very high on my life's checklist of things to do—in the top five for sure. Now I was sitting on this kinky old brightly-but-badly painted bus next to a wonderful open window that let me lean half of my body out if I wanted to. Our seats were big and high and the bus was crowded—full of Pakistanis and "Hippie Trail to India" travelers.

I was glad to get out of Kabul and almost immediately we were in a scenic mountain pass. From here to the border, while nothing by Pacific Northwest standards, was the closest thing to lush that we've seen in Afghanistan. We even passed a lake, but I saw no boats. I wondered how many, or how few, Afghans had ever been in a boat.

We stopped in Jalalabad for a hurried lunch break and we were back on the road in 20 minutes. We were nearing the border and apprehension grew. We hoped it wouldn't be too much of a hassle but by now nothing surprised us.

The Afghanistan border station, while time consuming, was easy. We just sat around eating a melon and wishing we had money for a Coke. Actually, we had planned our cash reserves very nicely and were leaving with no afghanis. Doing this is both a game and a money-saving skill among travelers. We waited our turn to be searched, filled out the form, got our passports stamped—the usual process—and loaded back on, only to stop 100 yards later for our introduction to Pakistan.

This place was pretty unruly. We piled into a room and one by one we were called up to the desk. The customs official "hunt and pecked" our vital statistics into his register and stamped our passports.

Passports in hand, we knew we were just halfway through the process but we weren't sure where to go next. We wandered into one ramshackle building and in a dark room, two men jumped up from

Hustlers sell whatever drug you'd like—with bus window service—at the Afghanistan-Pakistan border.

two cots and welcomed us to lie down. No thanks! We got out of there and were overrun by dope dealers and black market money-chargers. Everything was so open and blatant that it almost seemed legal. We bought $10 worth of Pakistan rupees and then tried to get our bags searched so we'd be done. Frustrated in the chaos, we just got on the bus and skipped the baggage check. At our window we were entertained by lots of hash sellers and a particularly persistent man with a small bottle of cocaine—4 grams for $30. I took his picture and told him to get lost.

Finally, we were loaded and ready to do it—to cross the Khyber Pass. I was thrilled. Physically, it was just like any other rocky mountain pass, but when you've wondered, dreamed, and thought about something for many years, it becomes special. Up and up the bus climbed. Hanging out the window, I tried to take in everything—every wild turn in the road, every fortress-crowned hill, every stray goat, every gaily painted truck that passed us, and every mud hut. I looked at the rugged people who inhabited this treacherous pass and wondered who they were, how they lived, what stories could they tell. Dry, rocky graveyards with wind-tattered flags littered the hillsides. Clouds threatened. We were moving out of the arid Arab side of South Asia and into the wet Indian subcontinent. From now on we would feel muggy—but enjoy the green countryside.

We crossed the Khyber Pass and passed through a tribal village to pay a toll for the privilege. I could see the men around with rifles ignoring the bus and gathered in circles trading both goods and stories…or perhaps conspiring.

In a few minutes we were in Peshawar and found that a direct train to Lahore was leaving in an hour. We saw nothing to keep us in Peshawar and the magnetism of India was getting stronger and stronger as we got nearer and nearer. We hassled around trying to decide how, what, and where to buy our tickets. This was a new experience—learning how to handle the Pakistani train system. A little bewildered and not sure what was our best move, we bought a $3.50 ticket (first class) for the 12-hour journey, wolfed down a quick 60-cent dinner, and found a spot on the not-so-classy first-class car.

The only difference between first and second class was padded seats and $1.50. We figured for 12 hours it would be nice to have the pads. Our car was very crowded. I was happy to be near a window that blew in hot, muggy air. We pulled out at 5:50, almost on time, and I savored the breeze.

For centuries, camel caravans, armies, and travelers have crossed from Afghanistan to Pakistan over the fabled Khyber Pass.

Khyber Pass—where trucks rumble and back-packers celebrate a milestone on the Hippie Trail to Kathmandu.

Leaving Afghanistan on the Khyber Pass, we passed through Waziristan, long a virtually ungovernable "autonomous region" where Pashtun tribes made their own rules and handled their own defense.

In Peshawar, the leading Pashtun city, people walked around with rifles slung over their shoulders.

The countryside was flat, lush, and interesting. After a while, I began reading Orwell's Animal Farm. It was good and the time passed nicely. Then it got dark and the bugs came. The lights worked like on my old bike—the faster you go, the brighter they shine. This was not a very bright train. The bugs took an unfortunate liking to me and I made a bloody declaration: "Death by ruthless squashing to any bug that lands on me from now on." I decided that I would just mash them with my thumb or fingers and roll them through my arm and leg hairs until they disappeared—either rubbing into my skin or falling off.

The ride dragged on and so did the bugs. We decided to break up the ride to Lahore at Rawalpindi, the halfway spot, and catch an early train in the morning to complete the trip.

It was nearly midnight as we stepped into the muddy puddled streets of Rawalpindi. There was a 5:15 train to Lahore in the morning so we could catch a good four hours of sleep—if we could catch a hotel. It looked very bad—every one was full and other people looking for a place were also frustrated. Luckily, I found a guy with a single open and a shower next door (Gene didn't tell me about the lizards until later). Otherwise, it was a hole barely worth the 10 rupees ($1) we paid. But it did serve its purpose. I took a cooling shower and found a comfortable spot among the bumps and curves of my cot and soon I had worked myself to sleep. Today was a good day—lots of miles covered, a new country, and I had crossed the Khyber Pass.

Saturday August 5:
Rawalpindi to Lahore, Pakistan

At 4:00, as we requested but didn't count on, the hotel guy woke us up. It wasn't a lot of sleep but was much better than a night in that buggy train and now we were prepared to finish the journey. Today I was high-spirited—that long road was nearing its end. In a few hours we would be at the last city in Pakistan, only minutes from the Indian border.

Our train was waiting. I had some nice little cakes and a couple of cups of tea on the platform and then Gene and I took our seats in the delightfully empty first-class car. What a great move we made getting out of that other train. It was risky—there may not have been a hotel or another timely train to catch or this one could have been late or overcrowded, but nothing like that happened. Everything worked out very nicely.

We pulled out at the 5:15 crack of dawn and I'm glad we got to roll through the countryside during the day—it was nice. I finished Animal Farm—good book—and then began reading up on India as the train filled. By the time we arrived in Lahore (noon) the train was packed and Gene and I were lucky to have seats. We got our first taste of beggars, cripples, religious singers, and crushing crowds that will be plaguing our train rides for the rest of the trip, but we got to our destination and that's what counts.

Lahore was a tangle of people, horses, strange vehicles, and hot, muggy noise. At first, we were lost without a map or anything, but we took a little funny three-wheeled motor rickshaw to the tourist info place and got what we needed plus a recommended moderately priced hotel. From now on, I think we'll seek out moderately priced or better hotels—live well, eat well, and stay healthy and happy.

We bounced and frolicked in a crazy rickshaw to the Hotel Menora and got a fine room for 62 rupees, or $6.50. It was clean, good service, fun, and had a great private toilet and shower—essential! At lunch I had communication problems and ended up eating two meals.

Okay, we were set up, we had eaten, and now we took a cab to the Badshahi Mosque, one of the largest in the world. The ride was crazy. We couldn't keep straight faces as we swerved in and out of traffic going both ways on all sides of the road. Later we worked our way through a herd of water buffalo or oxen that easily could have pounded our rickety rickshaw into a puddle if they wanted to. We made it though, paid the guy 3 rupees, and were appropriately impressed by the huge mosque that loomed before us.

Talking to people in Pakistan about their relationship with India, here's what I think I learned: When India won its independence from Britain it then had

In Lahore, we hung out with Pakistani med students in a park and shared perspectives.

to deal with a divided society with a Hindu majority and a Muslim minority that didn't want to share a nation. After tragic fighting, the Muslims established East and West Pakistan—Islamic havens cut from the eastern and western sides of India's vast territory. They eventually became Bangladesh and Pakistan, and India's aggressive Hindus pushed most of India's Muslims out of their Hindu-dominated country and into these new Muslim lands.

I'm glad we stopped in Lahore. After watching a changing of the guard that tried to be very impressive, I put on slippers and had a blanket wrapped around my indecent legs and we entered the vast courtyard of this Muslim holy spot. We climbed way up to the top of a minaret and got a spectacular view of low, flat, and sprawling Lahore. Careful not to trip over my modesty dress, I descended the spiral stairs and we crossed over to inspect the lackluster fort. I'm glad we took care of these sights today because now we know we can go to India tomorrow.

Rickshaw-ing through the chaos, we went to the main street called "The Mall" and spent a few early evening hours just wandering around, stopping for a bite to eat or to sip a Coke—just experience this cultural center of Pakistan.

Back in our hotel, we turned the fan up to about a gale and discussed what a wonder the saying "When the shit hits the fan" is. Later I proposed that in India we both work very hard to learn about and gain an understanding of the Hindu religion. That should give our visit a little more depth than just a tourist outing.

I really enjoyed our shower and for the first time in my life I was able to take a shower and pee into the toilet at the same time. I felt great. I don't know why I haven't gotten sick yet, but I'm not complaining.

Clean for the time being, I went downstairs for a Coke and to catch up in this journal and then get to sleep at a decent time.

Sunday, August 6: Lahore to Amritsar, India!

For some stupid reason, we were woken at 5:00 a.m. by the hotel guy in response to someone's complaint that we were roaming the hotel. Nonsense! And now we couldn't get any more good deep sleep. Later we got up and had breakfast. Boy, is this place hot and muggy. Even a shower and the fan doesn't hide the humidity and stickiness.

Before leaving Pakistan, we wanted to check out the Lahore Museum, so braving the almost hilarious traffic, we hopped into a three-wheeled rickshaw and went down to see it. Not a bad museum, but the English tour they advertised was "on leave." Oh well, we checked it out rather quickly, really enjoying a statue of the "Fasting Buddha," and then got antsy to get to India.

Lahore is a ramshackle, "thrown-together," crazy city cluttered with insignificant vehicles, businesses, and fruit stands. There's rarely a dull moment for the wide-eyed visitor. In the commotion, we found the bus station and waited for bus #12 for the Indian border. It's interesting to see where the trans-Asia tourists accumulate. This was one place where, predictably, many brightly colored backpacks were found in a sea of dirty canvas brown.

We waited and waited for the bus. It was crucial for our spirits that we get into India today, and these borders are notorious for taking a lot of time and simply closing down for the day. A nice old guy offered us a cheap taxi ride to the border and we jumped on it. After 30 or 40 minutes of weaving in and out of cattle and wild traffic, we reached the end of Pakistan. The taxi wanted 25 rupees and we emptied our remaining 18 ½ into his hands and escaped, taking refuge in the customs house.

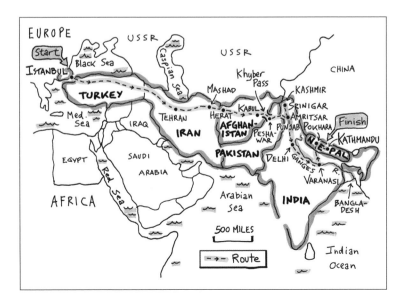

India: My dream realized!

Words can't explain my joy as I stepped across that happy tree-lined border. I dreamed so long to experience this enchanted sub-continent and now I was here. I could have flown. But I'm glad I endured the overland road even though there were many moments, long moments, when I thought the whole idea was a stupid mistake and I dreamed of the good fun and food I could be having in Greece or Italy. But now, as I walked among turbaned Sikhs, wallowing water buffalo, and lush green fields, I felt fantastic, beaming with a feeling of accomplishment, and my spirit soared.

I doubt if I'll ever do this trip this way again, but I experienced three rewarding and unforgettable weeks and learned so much about myself. I've turned the key and the world opened up before me, rekindling the flame that Europe was beginning to have trouble with.

After clearing customs, we hopped into a minibus for Amritsar. Before long, it was packed to the hilt and I knew this was India. Population density...and I liked it.

Amritsar, just across the border from Lahore, is the capital of the Punjab, the holy center of the Sikh religion and a jumbly city full of frantic bicycle rickshaws and people. We checked into the Tourist Guest House and got a large no-frills double with a fan for $2 or 20 rupees. Gene was still feeling lousy so he sacked out while I went out to arrange for our ticket to Kashmir. There was little point in walking when I could get doorstep-service in the rickshaws for pennies. I sat in the buggy part while a hard-working, but very eager guy happily pedaled me wherever I wanted to go.

We wanted to fly to Srinagar to save many hours of hassles and travel time. There were no flights available for several days so, rather desperate, I went to the station and got train tickets. Gene needed a good night's sleep but we also needed to get up to Srinagar. I grabbed the last first-class sleeper available on tonight's train to Jammu for Gene. I still needed a ticket for me and I went to work trying to just get on the train any way possible.

First class was sold out, there was one second-class reserved seat left but I had to get the ticket first before I could get the reservation and the second-class ticket booth was typically mobbed by Indians.

What to do? I desperately wanted that reserved seat to avoid the chaos of unreserved bottom-class train travel. I knew tourists often got preferred treatment so I made friends with the assistant station master and other key people and, after lots of running around, I had what I wanted. Gene's first-class sleeper cost 50 rupees and my second-class seat cost 9 rupees ($1) for the eight-hour journey. We would be leaving tonight so we'd have to give up our hotel room but, to me, that was no biggie.

Crossing the border into India, I strangely felt like I was coming home. Going from sparsely populated and arid to densely populated and humid, and from Islam to Hindustan, there was a clear feeling that we were crossing a big cultural divide.

I woke Gene up with the news and we had to wrap up our Amritsar sightseeing in a couple hours. We rickshawed over to the fantastic Golden Temple, the St. Peter's and Mecca of the Sikh religion. This was the most holy place for the Sikhs and they opened their doors with wonderful hospitality to anyone who visited.

We had to wear a scarf over our heads and enter barefoot after washing our feet. Inside the massive square complex was a man-made lake and, in the middle, as if it was floating, was a golden island of Sikh holiness.

We wandered around soaking in all the exotic rituals and friendly people. Inside the island I saw a mysterious and very serious gathering of pilgrims and holy people. Music was played by a small orchestra, people were tossing coins, meditating, and taking a sort of communion. I was quite surprised that we were allowed to experience this room. I'll never forget it.

After touring the Sikh Museum, we were done with Amritsar's only really big attraction, and Gene and I were happy to be pushing on tonight.

Back at the hotel, we rested and showered and caught a rickshaw over to the station. All the way I was busy counseling our rickshaw boy—a curious and very eager-to-learn Sikh—on how to hustle American girls. He learned to say, "How's it goin' baby?" by the time we got to the station.

I got my first sample of the famed Indian train-station food. I had a great meal of meat patties, fries, cooked vegetables, bread and butter, pudding, and a pot of tea filling me for well under a dollar. And that was the more expensive "Western" meal. You can live very cheap in India.

We had a bit of a panic trying to locate our reserved places but we managed. It was nice to see "Mr. Steves" written on the list outside the car. I said goodbye to Gene for the night as he settled into his first-class sleeper and I stepped into my second-class car to find seat #40. In the process I bumped into Maria and Duncan, our English friends from the Istanbul-Tehran ride. Two other veterans of that marathon were also on the train. Asia is a huge continent but us Hippie Trail overlanders seem to stick together. It was great to see my favorite people from that long ride again. We shared our adventures since we parted in Tehran and chatted for a while. They were lucky to have sleeping berths. Before I returned to my seat, I borrowed Maria's book on India and actually made several hours of the long ride interesting by diving into that book and getting a great background on India and Hinduism. With each stop of the train, I'd run out, soak my shirt, and have a quick Coke or tea. I kind of mentally turned the potential all-night-ordeal into an interesting personal challenge. And I carried out hundreds of death sentences on bugs that landed on me. Many will forever stain the pages of Maria's book.

Braving cockroaches and the unknown elements of the filthy floor of the train, I stretched out on my poncho for a troubled hour or two of half-sleep and at 4:30 we were in Jammu.

Travelers are warmly welcomed to visit the holiest place of the Sikhs, their Golden Temple in Amritsar, in Indian's Punjab region.

Monday   Aug 7th   Jammu – Srinagar, Kashmir

It was still dark as I groggily stepped off
e train. I was ho.... to be in Jammu because
at was half............. The all night
ain ride .... t by rather
uickly. I .... f together
d we .... station.
veryone .... escape the
ucky hear .... in the
lissful val.....

I stretched .... covered every
ch of my body with spare cloths to escape the
gs and slept for an hour while our friends
t us tickets for the 7:00 Srinagar bus.
What a smooth connection. By 7:15 we were
tting in the bouncy back seat of our rickity
t class" bus and for about $2.50 we would
pend 12 hours winding through treacherous
ountain roads to the hidden land of Kashmir.
Ooo! I was excited. Not even feeling my lack
sleep, I enjoyed the ride. The ....

CHAPTER 6

You're Now in Paradise—Kashmir

August 7-13

Monday August 7: Jammu to Srinagar, Kashmir

It was still dark as we groggily stepped off the train. I was happy to be in Jammu only because that was halfway to Srinagar. And the all-night train ride was over. Actually, it went by rather quickly. I rinsed my face and pulled myself together and we followed the crowd to the bus station. Everyone seemed to be headed north to escape the mucky heat of India and find happiness in the blissful valley of Kashmir.

I stretched out on the cement, covered every inch of my body with spare clothes to escape the bugs, and slept for an hour while our friends got us tickets for the 7 a.m. Srinagar bus.

What a smooth connection. By 7:15 we were sitting in the bouncy back seat of our rickety "A class" bus and for about $2.50 we would spend 12 hours winding through treacherous mountain roads to the hidden land of Kashmir.

Ooo! I was excited. Not even feeling my lack of sleep, I enjoyed the ride. The scenery was dramatic and I soaked up the fun conversation my British friends, Maria and Duncan, had to offer. I really enjoy something about Maria, but I guess that's just too bad.

Our bus was relatively controlled and made good time considering the age of the bus and the condition of the terrain we had to cross. It was 300 kilometers (nearly 200 miles) of almost continuously winding and switchback narrow roads spiced with dreadful cliffs, huge falling boulders, local natives, lots of trucks and military vehicles, and constant signs reminding drivers with tacky little rhymes and slogans like "Drive carefully—your family needs you" or "Better late than dead."

Kashmir, where India meets Tibet, is a wondrous place.

The neighborhood was filled with floating guesthouses for rent.

The countryside was lush and green—almost tropical. I knew right away that this was my kind of place. By mid-afternoon we went through a very long one-lane tunnel and when we popped out, we were greeted by a cheery sign saying, "Welcome to Kashmir—you're now in Paradise." Then we were struck by a view of the huge valley that substantiated the claim about paradise. This place was dreamy. The landscape was mystically beautiful like the fantastic fuzzy landscapes that typically make the background of paintings of the Madonna or the Mona Lisa. This valley, so far away from everything, was worthy of any praise anybody ever gave it.

The wild and windy road became a drive through a garden and I thought maybe Dubrovnik was being replaced by Kashmir as my ideal place for a romantic honeymoon.

After a couple more hours, we pulled into Srinagar, the Venice of North India, and just like the guides warned, we were swamped by very desperate houseboat owners eager to rent their cheap places to stay. Fighting our way through, determined to just get some info first, we got a map and a guide and then we were claimed by one "boat lord" and whisked away in a three-wheeled scooter to the dock where we sat in a luxurious, long water taxi, kind of like a Venetian gondola with a canopy bed on it.

This guy offered us the world, including a free first night to check his boat out. We did, and while it was nice and cheap, we didn't really like the pressure job he put on us and we wanted to check out a few more places. I hailed a boat and with some difficulty, we excused ourselves to get a more thorough review of the Srinagar scene.

Muzaffar's, our floating—and luxurious for us—home in Kashmir.

Several boats down the way, we stopped at a cute looking houseboat with a vacancy sign out. The neighbor boats had very, very comfortable laid-back and relaxed-looking tourists just laying around and enjoying the leisurely life that abounds here. The owner came running over and we were quite impressed by his boat and his style. He gave us the old line about the secret price he would give us and we pretended to be impressed—not really caring too much about the price as much as about the quality. We read the rave reviews some of his previous American guests gave him and agreed to the healthy price of 80 rupees for the double with dinner, breakfast, tea, and a family of literal servants. I knew we were giving him a very good price but I also knew that when you pay well for something like this, you reap the benefits of a truly first-class product.

Sitting topside on the sundeck, Gene and I sipped tea with crackers as the red sky darkened and boats of all kinds glided quietly by below us.

This was what I had dreamed of and what I had been waiting for. Twenty-five days ago, I left rainy Savonlinna in the middle of Finland and I knew I had a long road to travel. Even then, my sights were set on Srinagar in the northwest corner of India. Now I'm sitting in my houseboat, sipping my tea, and I will be very busy from now on, just relaxing and enjoying myself. Never have I worked so hard or traveled so long for a single moment. And this perch in enchanting Kashmir was well worth it.

Then the boy stopped by to tell us that the hot water was prepared and we could shower before our duck dinner was ready. After our showers, we were presented with roast duck, cooked potatoes, carrots, rice, sweet and cooked apples in syrup, a wonderful Persian tea, and water that the man said he boiled and was safe to drink. We stuffed ourselves while the man stood next to the table beaming with pride for the meal and making sure that our every need was attended to. That all made me a bit uncomfortable, but India is a culture of hard class divisions and

Tea time!

staying here, you've got servants whether you want them or not. This was a family show and I guess this one family had run this houseboat for generations—probably serving rich British bureaucrats who ruled India back in the 1800s.

As boats paddled by, crickets chirped, and Kashmiris argued noisily across the canal, I sat in the living room sipping sweet Persian tea and collecting my thoughts in this journal. I'm looking forward to becoming at-home in Kashmir.

Tuesday, August 8: Srinagar

I slept exactly eight good hours and got up for breakfast alone. Gene was going to just have a quiet morning. After I had my hot cereal with oat milk, toast, egg, and tea, I caught a shikara (Kashmiri gondola) to the "mainland" and then went down to the Air India office to book our tickets down to Delhi and then on to Nepal. (I can enjoy myself more at any destination when I've done the work to prepare for a smooth and efficient departure.) I found the flights with the correct dates and great prices but I needed Gene's passport. Oh well.

Our fruits and vegetables came to us.

I made the trip back to our houseboat, ok'd the plan with Gene, got his passport, and returned to the office to find it very noisy and crowded. I made my way to the desk and got two youth tickets for Srinagar-Delhi on the 14th and Delhi to Grokapur on the 18th. Each ticket with the 25% youth discount was about $30 totaling $115. That was great. We'd save so many difficult days on the ground. Imagine—only one hour to fly to Delhi versus several days of bus and train otherwise. I would have preferred flying to Kathmandu in Nepal but that cost triple the price of the flight to Gorakhpur which was still in India but only a short ride to the Himalayan kingdom.

I came home the long way, having a little boy paddle me through the many canals lined with houseboats of all classes—from half-sunk, rotten rafts to virtual floating palaces. Most of them were very nice.

After I got back, I joined Gene up on the roof and under the sun and we had some delicate Persian tea with Kashmiri bread for a snack. The other people on our boat had checked out and now we had the boat to ourselves and we moved into the best room with that all-important sit-down toilet. This boat life is great. At $5 each for boat and board, we're paying a very good price. Our friends got the works for half that and we could have chiseled on the price but how could we complain. I like to feel like I'm paying a good price because then I can command a good return. I like to ask for plenty of tea, get my filthy clothes washed, be able to borrow the shikara (little boat) when I want it, and still feel like I'm making a family's day financially.

Our houseboat has a little veranda overlooking the canal, a richly furnished living room with a small dining table, two double bedrooms, and two bathrooms, and on top is a pleasant sun deck where we can watch the Kashmiri world float by. Boats, long and narrow, laden with anything you could want, float by servicing anyone who wants service. You could spend weeks here and never leave the boat. Across the canal is a small jungle inhabited by a large local family and we can observe life going on the way it has for centuries. Birds and bats fly by, dark tanned naked children paddle happily through the lily pads, and out back the owner and his family live in a modest little boat quite apart from our touristy world, but ready to do whatever we ask. I hope this lifestyle doesn't permanently corrupt me. (It's worth the risk.)

Gene and I borrowed the ancient shikara, got a second paddle, and set out to explore Lake Dal. At first, the going was hard and slow. We were fighting a bit of a current and neither of us were very good with this neat but difficult old boat. Little boys floated by solo, paddling faster than the both of us but this was great. We were on our own, free to mosey in and out of lagoons lined with traditional boat families doing their fascinating thing. The nicest thing about it was no one could try to help us or sell us things—we were unpestered…and free to explore.

Working hard, we made our way through the houseboat neighborhoods and out into Lake Dal. We docked on a "swimming boat." A guy "parked" our boat for us and we stripped down to our underwear and enjoyed a fun, if not refreshing, swim. The water was so warm—I was actually cooler in the shade. I went for a fantastic round of water skiing. What a thrill, waterskiing under the lush Himalayas and the Kashmir blue skies. I skied with abandon and had a blast whipping along to the side of the speed boat, jumping the wake, and going around and around. Later I tried and failed to get up on one ski. I tried getting up on two and kicking one off but failed miserably. I could feel the altitude here—I was exhausted. After lounging around and splitting an apple juice (we paid 30 rupees—$3.50—for the services there), our boat was fetched, and off we rowed.

The shikara drew only a few inches and had no keel so we had a hard time steering a straight course. Every few minutes we'd clumsily do a 360-degree circle, probably much to the entertainment of the local boaters nearby. We checked out a garden isle, bought an apple from a floating general store, enjoyed the novel experience of having a nude and beautiful girl frolicking around our stern, and then as the sun set, we returned home, tired, a bit sunburned and ready for dinner.

Back home I enjoyed tea on the roof and then we were served chicken, potatoes, a local cousin of potato, stewed plums, tea, and boiled water for dinner.

Wednesday, August 9: Srinagar

We slept in and had the typical houseboat breakfast. Today I planned to get my shopping out of the way. Shopping on the road is kind of a necessary evil. I think it's nearly criminal to waste travel days in little touristy shops but in a way it's part of the trip. I just want to do it quick and get it over with.

I made my way through several pitiful beggars to the bank where I changed $150 and then I walked through Srinagar seeing what it had to offer. This was the first time I had been in the actual city and it was a fun place— lots of Indians there on vacation in all different local outfits, inviting parks, chaotic intersections, plenty of street sellers, and more than enough craft shops. I browsed through a bookstore for a while, picking up a learn-to-spell book that looked like it mite work, and then I made my way to the Government Central Market.

The Central Market was 60 or 80 shops in a large square all with fixed and government-regulated prices. I didn't have the energy today to do a lot of bargaining, so this was my safest bet. I slowly made the rounds, running the Indian gauntlet of vicious storekeepers and craftsmen. Take a look, take a little look, take a look, look, look!!!

A lot of the stuff did nothing for me. It was "Pier One Import" kitsch. I did find some handwoven pillow covers, papier mâché boxes, and silver stuff I liked but I bought nothing yet. It's important to "feel out" the market first.

I had to meet Gene at the tourist reception center at 2:30 so I made my way back, really enjoying a cold apple juice and the crazy side streets of Srinagar.

At the Tourist Center, Gene, Maria, and Duncan were waiting. I showed up and we did a little business and went out for lunch. We found a very Indian coffeehouse and had a tasty little meal for a pittance. Having coffee sparked my coffee tasters and I realized how long it had been since I had a good cup of "joe."

Gene wasn't really in the market for shopping but I wanted to be done with it today. I got myself psyched to just buy, buy, buy, and we made our way to the Central Market. On the way, we made a provisions stop, picking up cough syrup for Gene, toilet paper, and toothpaste. Toilet paper costs a lot here—50 cents a scrawny roll, but American products manufactured in India are dirt cheap—15 cents for a small toothpaste.

At the market I ushered Gene through the pleading merchants to my favorite shops and went wild buying things. I got three lovely hand-woven pillow covers with neat, deep colors and happy patterns (I'm thinking a little bit domestically for post-college life), several cute little papier mâché hand-painted boxes (a local specialty), another little fox fur "purselette" that, when draped around my chin, makes a crazy full beard that matches my hair, and some silver

jewelry. Now that was done and I had made several friends in the market. We hurried back to the houseboat and ordered dinner.

We dropped by Maria's and Duncan's boat to invite them to drop by for tea and go with us to the Shalimar Gardens sound-and-light show, but she was waiting for a custom-made shirt to be delivered and couldn't go.

Now that we were leaving, our boat man was cutting back on the service. In fact, the servants were almost mutinous. We asked him to send a shikara to pick up our friends and he refused! Our dinner was a rather meager stew with old bread. Afterward, he nearly dictated what he wanted me to put into his guest-book—good food, great friends, etc. I graciously managed to write a simple thank you without going into elaborate and exaggerated praise. Then I paid him 240 rupees ($30) for three days and he had the nerve to ask for laundry money. That killed my last respect for him. I thought he had class, but he was getting on me. I had to keep our relations good though because we wanted to leave our luggage there for a few days.

Now we took a boat ashore and headed for the sound-and-light show. It was hard to get a taxi or rickshaw to take us out there for a reasonable price. A three-wheeler finally agreed to take us 13 kilometers out to the gardens, wait, and bring us back for 25 rupees. With no time to bicker, we got in and we jumbled along Lake Dal to the famous and romantic Shalimar Gardens. We were 10 minutes late, foolishly bought first-class tickets (it didn't make any difference—just cost double), ran to our seats, and quickly sank back into the Mughal Empire (1600s) and lights and sound brought the sexy garden dreamily alive. The moon shone, the trees were silhouetted, and colorful lights and historic stories help me imagine what these gardens might have been like before the arrival of Europeans. It was quite nice, but too short. I really enjoyed the light work, fountains, and Indian music.

Our little three-wheeled rickshaw was waiting at the door and we headed home. Halfway there, I had him stop, shut off the motor, and we sat in lovely silence on the moonlit bank of Lake Dal. This is a very special valley and I will return.

My favorite crazy singing and jabbering shikara boy took us home, but I did most of the paddling while he told me all about his lucky raffle tickets. Reaching our once-friendly houseboat a thought hit me: It's funny, when you're treated like a king you begin to expect it and when the servants let you down, it takes a little bit of adjusting.

It was late and we hit the sack.

Thursday, August 10: Srinagar to Gulmarg

We had to arise early this morning. I had a pretty lousy cold, trickling shower and we had a meager breakfast. I can't believe how the quality disappears once we've paid and are leaving. The houseboat servant was kind of pouting because we weren't staying with him. The breakfast was meager, stale, and there was no porridge. Oh well, we left most of our stuff and took just two small rucksacks to the tourist reception center where we caught our 9:00 bus to the mountain town of Gulmarg.

This was a "tourist" bus so a token worthless commentary came with it. Latitude, longitude, elevation, and population…just the facts. It was like the guide memorized an encyclopedia entry for the place. We were climbing from 5,200 feet to 8,700 feet on this nice bus filled mostly with Indian tourists. It is interesting to observe the Indian tourists that flock to Kashmir. There are tons of tourists here, but very few are European. That's nice, but I think we get "hit up" harder.

The two-hour ride was a pleasant little hop for us after our long trans-Asia bus experience. Soon we climbed into a lush forest crawling with monkeys. It's so great to see monkeys wild in the forest! They would look at the bus and then scamper away—often with a baby clinging to their back.

By 11:00 we pulled into Gulmarg and the hungry natives were ready. Screaming and running alongside the bus, scores of men ready to make the quick and easy tourist buck attacked the bus even before the tourists got out. It was somewhere between funny and scary. No one could hear the final tourist guide commentary over the screaming local people. We didn't really want to step into that mob, and we waited on the bus until it cooled down a bit and then stepped into India's high mountain resort—Gulmarg.

Before us, past the aggressive "pony men," stretched the hilly green meadows of lovely Gulmarg. A very nice place, nestled in the mountains and really "away from it all."

We walked stubbornly through the mass of locals and oriented ourselves, checking out a few hotels and planning our day. After a great meal at the Kingsley Hotel, we set out to ride up to Khilanmarg high above even Gulmarg at 10,000 feet.

All the pony men gathered noisily around us, showing cards and credentials. We chose an old man assisted by a young man and had to accept their 20-rs-per-pony price to go up to Khilanmarg and back. One thing I insisted on was to get the pony and no pony man, so my guy got to stay in Gulmarg while I took his pony. I checked the horse out, making sure that, with my very limited experiences, I could handle her. Everything seemed fine, so we set out. Gene got a more difficult horse and the old man followed us, which turned out to be nice because the trail was a bit ambiguous and the old man was a little security for us.

I was a bit cautious on my horse. I broke my arm once falling off a pony and I was carrying my camera and zoom lens which would never survive a fall. There was no horn on the saddle but it offered a little flap to hang on to the reins. I got my horse, Ginger, to gallop and it was really thrilling. In a canter, I was popping up and down like a cross between a pogo stick and a jackhammer. What fun! Then we began to climb and the trail got muddy and rocky. The going was slow and difficult and I had this terrible image of Ginger slipping, falling, and crushing my leg beyond recognition. We made our way up the lousy trail through fantastic scenery and after four kilometers, we reached Khilanmarg. The old man got a tow most of the way up hanging onto Gene's pony's tail.

Khilanmarg, at 10,000 feet, was rugged beauty—an open meadow high above the placid valley of Kashmir and bordered by towering mountains. Cows grazed among the rocks and a few trees and rustic shacks, and there were three or four tents set up to serve the tourists tea or coffee. There were about six or seven other tourists up there—all were Indian.

The clouds kept us from viewing the Himalayas and Nanga Parbat, the world's ninth-highest mountain. We sat under the tent through a short rainstorm. Gene had Nescafé and I ate some peanuts we've been carrying since Afghanistan. Then, unencumbered by camera equipment or lousy trails, Ginger and I went galloping happily across the meadows—unforgettable; if I only had a little more confidence, it would have been even better.

On the far side of the meadow, I came to a cozy-looking dwelling made of stacked stones. I couldn't pass it up. I rode up and was greeted by the beautifully natured family and I made myself at home. Stepping inside, I entered a fascinating world. Not a trace of the 20th century could be found, nor the 19th or 18th. Really! This was a pure look at life in the wilds. The father was sleeping on leaves but woke up with a gleam in his eyes and a warm handshake. The mother, who looked much older than she was but totally healthy, was kneading bread next to an earthen fire that filled the hut with a warm, smokey feeling and a good smell. Rays of light shone through cracks in the rocks landing on the happy faces of the long-haired and freckled children. Their clothes were dirty and their hair was unwashed, but nothing struck me as unclean. I'll never forget sitting on the log under the thatched roof next to the beautiful teenage girls and in front of the little fireplace-stove. It seemed like a comfortable existence. Animal pelts hung on a tree outside, sleds were quietly awaiting the first winter snowfall, and I imagine they would remember my visit as long as I would.

The only problem with the whole experience was we had not one word in common; they were totally detached from any outside influence, yet they were quite aggressively after bakshish. I ended up handing out about 5 rupees, or 60 cents.

I took one last gallop on Ginger, and Gene and I decided to pay off the old man and walk back down on our own. This would be more leisurely for us, we

---

I've never met a family so disconnected from the rest of the world...or so warm and welcoming.

figured safer, and I dreaded making that poor little pony carry me down the steep miserable trail.

Now we frolicked our way down to Gulmarg, soaking in this great nature, looking for but not finding monkeys and having to rest often because of the thin air at 10,000 feet. It was densely cloudy but the temperature was perfect.

By 4:00, we were back in Gulmarg, and we lazed around checking out a little Hindu temple and then went back to the Kingsley Hotel and took a nice room with a royal view of the valley and the big hopping black birds for 20 rupees ($2.50). We had hard beds, warm blankets, hot water, and a sit-down toilet. What more could we ask for at about $1 each?

After a pot of tea, we ordered dinner. We've been learning more and more about the food and have been enjoying the Indian cuisine. Rice, dal (a lentil-type soup), chapati (thin, round breads), vegetable pakora (kind of like onion rings), mutton or chicken prepared in various ways, soups, boiled weird veggies, and lots of tea. We ate very well tonight for about a buck a piece.

In the lounge area, we met two very well-traveled guys, a Canadian and Daniel, a Swiss man. We spent the night sharing information and travel stories, and I couldn't stop the conversation to do my writing. Those guys got me so excited about India, the far East, and all my future travels. They also had very encouraging news about the availability of cheap plane tickets back to Europe.

The night brought the chill and that sent me upstairs and under my heavy blanket. It was then that I realized I was very tired—and a little saddle-sore.

Friday, August 11: Gulmarg to Nagin Lake

Daniel, Gene, and I enjoyed eggs, porridge, toast, and tea for breakfast, and then we headed out. The weather still hid the mountains as we said goodbye to Gulmarg and the pony men and began the walk down to Tangmarg. We chose to walk the several kilometers down rather than hitch in hopes of seeing more monkeys. We made our way down the steep trail but saw only big birds, cows, pony people and their ponies, and a stray villager here and there. Nevertheless, the walk was very beautiful.

A cloud burst sent us scurrying under a big tree with the Kashmiris who were also hiking in the area. This was a good chance for us to stare at them and for them to stare at us as we all got dripped on. The trail became a muddy river and the rain poured down with monsoon force.

After about 15 minutes it stopped, we left our umbrella-tree, and hiked on downhill into busy little Tangmarg just in time to crowd onto the local bus back to Srinagar. They just don't build their buses with any leg room around here and my knees were screaming all the way back to Srinagar.

Rather than exploring the valley, we decided to check out old Srinagar and Nagin Lake today—maybe finding a very peaceful houseboat on that lake to sloth-out on.

First on our agenda, however, was to find a decent restaurant and fill up. I was starved. We caught a little three-wheeler, rode until we found a good-looking place, and sat down to eat. We ordered a feast for about a dollar each. The most expensive part of any meal is the bottled soft drinks.

Satisfied, we stepped out and into a funny cross between a three-wheeler and a bus. It was a big three-wheeler that sat 10 people, 30 in a pinch. We headed out to Ali Kadal—the old Srinagar.

Old Srinagar was exciting, colorful, full of busy and lazy people, and a trip just to walk through. We ambled aimlessly, capturing innumerable memories. This is where old men sat cross-legged in doorways that look like windowsills, engulfed in their big Korans (Kashmir is mostly Muslim), boys climbed like monkeys around streetlamps and roof tops, cows munched newspapers in the streets, and onion-sellers handled mobs of hungry customers.

The buildings were ornately carved wood, aged and darkened after countless hot summers and violent winters. Mosques rose above the tangled skyline and trembling bridges crossed Jhelum River. (I have a hunch that sharing these experiences and describing these sights adequately, even with the help of photographs, will be frustrating.)

We wandered into a neighborhood of ramshackle houses, torn-apart streets, dusty horses and what looked to me like ruins left by a war. Not wanting to linger there, we walked to the edge of town where we were met by a long-bearded, dignified old gentleman who spoke very good English. He introduced himself saying he wasn't a businessman, he worked for the hospital. Then he showed us a photograph of him from the 1940s in the hospital. After walking with us for a while, he gave us the pitch we should have known was coming, and I signed his book donating 2 rupees to the hospital.

It was hot, we were tired, and there we stood under the impressive hill topping Srinagar fort, just outside the city and several kilometers from Nagin Lake. Then, out of the blue clip-clopped a tonga with two guys offering us a ride to Nagin Lake. We hopped in and a few minutes later, we got out and we were on the shores of peaceful and beautiful Nagin Lake and ready to find us a first-class houseboat.

After several "Sorry, we're full"s and getting a feeling like this lake was for diplomats, rich Germans, and honeymooners only, we found "The Ritz." On the outside it was nothing special, lacking the highly varnished, ornately carved exterior of other boats, but inside it was lavish and spacious—really the Ritz. We were impressed with the peaceful location in the marshy shore of Nagin Lake among high reeds and lots of birds, with a gorgeous view of the fort and the mountains. Inside we had a spacious double bedroom with soft beds, full bath, Western toilet, fancy carved wood paneling, Persian carpet, mirrors, and a view. The dining room was nice, with high royal-type chairs, plenty of boiled drinking water, fine dishes, and, of course, a view. The living room was just as

Kashmir, while part of India, is mostly Muslim rather than Hindu.

Following in the vacation footsteps of yesterday's Indian elites: backpackers enjoy the relative luxury, peace, and cool of Kashmir.

good with comfortable chairs and a sofa, lots of books and magazines, and a sunny back patio. The servants had enough class to serve well but not get in the way. While they were fun to talk to and be friends with, they sensed when we wanted to be private. I was shown the old guest book and this boat has a history going back to the 1920s, and this family has been in the houseboat business for much longer than that.

We had tea up on the sun deck and I just really got into the ever-changing Kashmiri world around us. All kinds of boats glided by. I got a roll of toilet paper from one merchant. We watched birds dive-bomb for fish and ducks paddle by. Shikaras and boats of all kinds ornamented the lake and, as the sun set, they became romantic silhouettes under a streaky pink-orange sky. We enjoyed the view until the moon shone brightly.

Dinner was ready and the servants thoughtfully described the Kashmiri food to us, explaining, for instance, that the spinach was not really spinach but a local vegetable much spicier and more packed with iron. I took an after-dinner snooze, wrote for a while, and went to bed early.

I'm determined to relax and restore my energy to 110%, because from the minute we land in Delhi on August 14th to the minute we board our plane in Frankfurt on September 8th, I will be going full-bore and taking in as much as I possibly can. But for now, this is my rest, this is Kashmir. It's my vacation and I will sleep in for as long as I want.

Saturday, August 12: Nagin Lake

An incredibly wicked monsoon storm—tons of rain and lightning—woke us at 4:00, but it soon subsided and I returned to my especially good dreams. Later, I woke up but had no desire to do anything but lie in bed and feel warm. In this coolness it's nice to need a blanket. I've had so many hot and naked nights. I think a human sleeps better when covered.

After our breakfast, we did nothing. Today is the nothing day. Intensive nothing and relaxation. I laid up on the sun deck, cooled off under the shower, laid in bed to dry, wrote a postcard or two, flipped through some old Newsweeks in the living room, and sat on the steps heading down to the water from the back deck looking at little fish and watching ducks gobble them up.

I didn't know we were getting lunch with our 100-rupees-a-day payment, but when they asked me what time I wanted it I said, "1:00, please." The lunch was the best meal so far, with tender goat meat and cooked vegetables. I sighed after completing the meal and had to lie down for a short rest. Gene and I talked about doing something like a shikara ride or a walk, but for the time being, that was very unlikely. I opened my window and let the sun warm my bed, motionless.

It was difficult, but after tea I put my shoes on and we stepped outside. I picked and peeled a barely ripe apple and we checked out the very huffy and selective Nagin Club. You had to be a "bona fide" tourist to join. We weren't impressed.

School let out as we walked down the street and we found ourselves in a parade of children. At the end of the lake, we caught a shikara ride back to "The Ritz" and spent the remainder of the afternoon reading, writing, sunbathing, and just enjoying the fantastic setting we found ourselves in. Dinner was served at 8:00 and as promised, we got our roast duck and it was great—really tasty.

I was struck at last with "loose stools." I never expected to last this long, and now, with confidence, I expect to be solid again soon. I took two Lomotil and tomorrow I'm on tea and boiled rice until I'm "myself" again.

As you might expect, I did nothing much for the rest of the evening and went to bed early. This day was great and from now on out it will be go, go, go. I have a lot of India to see before September 8th.

Sunday, August 13: Srinagar

We slept in and had a nice, if bland, breakfast and I began my bland, anti-diarrhea diet. I learned it in Syria last year and it works great: basically bread, rice, and tea until I'm solid again.

We checked out of the Ritz. I fulfilled my obligation of writing praises in their guestbook, but after paying the 100 rupees ($12) for the second day, I refused to give further bakshish—100 rupees was enough. That soured our last moments at the Ritz and we walked away not wanting to look back.

(All along this Hippie Trail there was a tension over prices and it was getting old. Even scruffy backpackers like us had more money than most locals. There was a local standard of gouging Westerners whenever possible. And we needed to be sure our money would last as long as our trip. So, I guess this playful battle between us and locals when we were buying things was just part of life on the road. We assumed their anger with us not paying their inflated prices was part of the show and we did our best to stay good natured about it all. While it got tiresome, it did get me thinking about the similar gap between people in the First World and in the Third World. The main thing: money was like gas in our tank. And if we ran out, we couldn't get home.)

A full bus came by and we squeezed in, making it even fuller. Standing in the aisle was tough because I was about two feet too tall, but for 40 paise (5 cents) it beat a taxi.

Back in Srinagar, we returned to houseboat Muzaffar intending to have a cheap night. We agreed to pay 35 rupees for a bed and big breakfast, we checked through our luggage, finding everything OK, and after a pot of tea, we took off to enjoy the famous gardens that visitors to Kashmir have been enjoying for centuries.

The tour bus was booked up so that meant it would be just us and the overflow bus. Actually, this was better—much cheaper, and we were totally free to come and go as we pleased. Our first stop was the famous Shalimar Gardens. In this lush valley, this colorful park of gardens, flowers, and tumbling water stood out. It was interesting to see all the Indians—both local and tourists from the south—coming here to relax and picnic. Next, after a short bus ride, we were at Nishat Gardens. Built by and fit for a royal king, I can imagine all the romantic hanky-panky that must have gone on around here. We took a snooze but soon the ants were playing Gulliver with me. After a nice cake and tea, I got a diarrhea attack and, in frantic silence, I found a hidden corner of the garden and fertilized.

Working our way around Lake Dal back to Srinagar, our next stop was the lavish Oberoi Palace Hotel. Many hotels put the word "palace" in their name, but only a few deserve such fanfare, and the Oberoi is one. We marched in like we belonged and snooped around. There was a 30-rupees minimum in the restaurant so the only thing we could afford was the wonderful bathrooms. I took a great roll of toilet paper for the good of our world and we said goodbye to the palace that can make you and one other a king for $60 a day including meals.

Back at the houseboat, I enjoyed watching the lake life go by: The French couple next to us rolling suspicious-looking cigarettes and feeding breadcrumbs to hungry ducks, two men pulling a clumsy houseboat down the canal, the local family across the way carrying on like there were no tourists and this wasn't the 20th century, and big carnivorous birds making the wispy trees sway. You could never leave this perch and write poems all day.

For dinner, we took a happy shikara ashore and found a popular restaurant where we filled ourselves vegetarian-ly for 75 cents each before returning to our boat to enjoy the comfortable place and talk with the Indian-American photographer who was sharing the Muzaffar houseboat with us. He is doing India on film and I enjoyed his pictures and learning something about photography from him.

Well, tonight's our last night here in Kashmir and we're both ready to get on with our trip. Tomorrow we kick off the last phase of this adventure.

CHAPTER 7

The Rain Poured Down—Delhi, India

August 14–17

August 14th, Monday   Srinagar – Delhi

We woke up for the last time in Kashmir happy to be
~~ing~~ out. After a disappointing breakfast the servant asked
"Food is good?" For on... ~~frank~~ + said, "Not really".
we packed ... ~~& ashore~~. I
~~anted~~ to do ... Emporium didn't
~~en~~ until 19... ~~post cards~~
wishing ...
At 11:00 ... ~~be ready to~~
~~ly~~ to Del... ~~t-town~~ but
~~e were~~ ... ~~avoid the long~~
~~ing overland~~
As I went ... they asked me if
had a knife. I did ... to check it separately. It
~~as~~ funny to say that just like another piece of baggage
~~s say~~ goodbye to it hoping I would see my dear Swiss
army knife again in Delhi. It joined the small pile
of Samurai swords, toy pistols + small knives – all
potential hi-jacking tools.
Our Boeing 737 was quite full as we took our seats
~~in~~ row 17 just behind the wing. I wondered just what
~~they meant~~ by "snacks" will be served during the
~~flight. I could~~ ...

Monday, August 14: Srinagar to Delhi, India

We woke up for the last time in Kashmir, happy to be flying out. We packed, said goodbye, and caught a boat ashore. I wanted to do a little shopping but the Government Emporium didn't open until 10:00 so Gene and I sat around writing postcards and wishing we had taken the early-morning flight.

At 11:00 our bus rolled out, packed with people ready to fly to Delhi. The airport was definitely "small-town," but we were tickled to be flying to Delhi and avoid the long, long over-land journey.

As I went through the security check, they asked me if I had a knife. I did and I had to check it separately. It was funny to tag that just like another piece of baggage and say goodbye to it hoping I would see my dear Swiss Army knife again in Delhi. It joined the small pile of Samurai swords, toy pistols, and small knives—all potential hijacking tools.

Our Boeing 737 was quite full as we took our seats in row 17 just behind the wing. I wondered just what they meant by "snacks" being served during the flight. I could use some big "snacks." We buckled up and by about 1:00 we were airborne and climbing through the puffy broken clouds and above our restful Kashmir Valley. We had a great week and now, rested, we are ready to finish the trip.

I felt particularly good watching the mountains below us flit easily by, thinking how nice it is not to be on a rickety old bus down there.

Snacks came—sandwich, cake, and apple juice—and I could have eaten more but one hour after we left, we were descending into the capital of India: Delhi.

They've been having the wettest monsoon in 70 years, and it was evident by the flooding we saw as we neared the ground. Then we vanished into a white cloud. I could see nothing but the wing out the window. It was scary to think we were going 400 miles per hour blind. Then we dropped below the clouds and landed with a loud rumble. A rear part of one of the jets flipped over, making a loud grinding noise, and I thought something was wrong, but apparently that is how the plane lands—and everything was fine as we pulled into our airport stall.

The rain poured down—this was Delhi and this was the monsoon season. I felt now like I was really in the heart of India—not the Punjab of the Sikhs or the Kashmir of the Muslims—but Hindustan, Delhi, the capital of India. Flooded rice fields, drenched dark Indians, and pampered cows lined the roads as we made our way to the center of Delhi.

We got out in the "Times Square" of modern India, Connaught Place, and ignoring the rain and the 85-degree temperature, we began our search for a plane ride to Europe. Like people told us, plane tickets were floating around everywhere. Lots of people offered us cheap Delhi-Europe flights right on the street. We went up into a few of the sleezy travel offices and were told good news—flights to London or Paris were $335 and Frankfurt for $380-400. They were consistent in their dates and prices, so they sounded reliable, but we couldn't be sure, and we would be a bit uneasy if we purchased a ticket from one of these shady agents. Air India or Pan-Am were no help to us, but we did find the Student Travel Bureau, and they could sell us reliable tickets at the same price. Now we had to decide which was better—flying to London on the 5th of September for $332 or to Frankfurt, on the 6th for $400. Plan #1 would give us two days in London, but we'd still have to buy the ticket to Frankfurt and we didn't know what that would cost. Plan #2 would be simpler, we'd have an extra day in India, but we'd have a dull day and a half to blow in Frankfurt. We will chew this over and probably decide on London by Wednesday.

With that completed, we worked on a hotel. Delhi wasn't a poor country town, and a decent place would cost us. We checked out several before we checked into the YMCA. A spartan double room, good bathrooms, and breakfast cost 43 rupees each ($5.40).

This place wasn't fancy and it was a huge drop from our luxurious Srinagar life, but it was clean, reasonable, in a good location, and we were tired, soaking wet, and eager to get out of the rain. In our room, we scattered our belongings everywhere to air and dry out. I took a lovely long shower and when 7:30 rolled around, we went downstairs and had a great $1.50 Western-style dinner. The waiters said the water was boiled and safe. I think it was just filtered, but it was so temptingly cold that we decided to drink it.

Curious to explore Delhi, we spent a few hours walking around this very quiet city of four million. Nothing was going on. We half-heartedly looked for a discotheque but we couldn't even find a juke box. We did find a movie theater, however, and we were just in time for the 9:45 show.

We paid our 3 rupees each and joined the happy gang of Indian moviegoers watch an "adults only" drama about a beautiful girl who gets her face burned ugly and falls in love with an Indian Frank Sinatra. The sex was totally left up to everyone's imagination, but the kiss and the girl's beautiful-but-clothed body were enough for the censors to classify it "dangerous for those under 18." It was melodramatic enough so that we could follow the Hindi plot without under-standing any of the conversation. It just went on and on and while we were quite entertained by it all, when we were let out for intermission at midnight, we never returned.

It was still very hot and muggy outside, as well as in our room. All of our stuff would stay humid as long as it stayed in Delhi. My beloved dead mink, which I named Her-rat, has started to smell a little and I don't know how I will dry her out.

With the fan blowing hot and muggy air on me, I fell asleep.

Tuesday, August 15: Delhi...and India's Independence Day

It's nice to have breakfast in the hotel. I like to be able to step downstairs for my Corn Flakes, toast, omelet, and tea. This hotel is great—everything is first class—except the rooms.

Today is India's Independence Day. 31 years ago, they broke away from England. We were hoping for an exciting day full of "Fourth of July"-type activi-ties, but there was nothing much going on—everything was just closed. We designed our day to see parks, monuments, and sights that were open all the time so we'd get something accomplished.

Starting down Parliament Road, we passed through the communications nerve center for India and then got to the Parliament building and the top

Traveling down Rajpath Road, we passed the Secretariat Buildings and Parliament building, on the way to Lodi Tombs Park.

governmental buildings. The was an impressive, expansive area full of parks and royal-type buildings. A long avenue, Rajpath, led to the famous India Gate with the eternal flame for WWI victims. We took a three-wheeled rickshaw to India Gate and were greeted by flexing cobras and dancing bears.

Memorial arches can be seen very quickly and we weren't in the mood for dancing bears, so we caught a rickshaw to the Lodi Tombs Park. This place was lovely. A very green park dotted with old, ruined tombs. We sat on a log and were entertained by cute little dressed-up and trained monkeys, and then wandered into a large group of Sikhs all dressed up at a religious picnic. Sikhs are amazing people—very productive, hardworking, prosperous, clean, proud, and devoted. They never cut their hair or beard but are sure to wash it every day. And they wear proud turbans, feel they have a strong bond wherever they are scattered, and in the Punjab, they dominate. They are quite evangelical and we got all the info we needed, so tonight for bedtime reading we will find out why we should be Sikhs.

After enjoying the choral group with the same wind-powered keyboard instrument and drums that we heard in the Amritsar temple, we left the gathering and caught a scooter to the zoo.

It's all happening at the zoo…Independence Day is a great day for the zoo. It was packed and festive. The monsoon clouds were gathering so everyone was busy enjoying the disappearing sun while they could. After some yummy "glucose" biscuits (my comfort snack here, so British and well wrapped for cleanliness) and a drink we paid 5 cents for, we went in. There were lots of exotic animals and even some ducks that came all the way from America! The problem was, we had to walk so far to see each animal. It was a vast yet sparsely populated zoo with sleepy hot animals scattered thinly around. I saw a tiger, peered right down a gross hippo's mouth—cavernous as a giant garbage can—and saw kangaroos hop just like in cartoons. Then the monsoon hit and everyone—animals and people—took refuge under the nearest tree and calmly waited for the rain to stop.

It did and we were really dragging in the hot, humid heat. I was so sweaty and sticky that, eventually, I wouldn't cross the lane for a unicorn. We caught a rickshaw to Connaught Place and went to the Kwality Restaurant expecting a kwality lunch.

Quite drained, we returned to our YMCA to sack out. There's just no escape from this heat and we just laid down on the beds in the middle of our mess and stared at our ceiling fans as they whirled on full speed.

Not really energetically but dutifully, we went out before dinner to walk around and check out the mysterious Jantar Mantar, a 200-year-old complex of huge astronomical measuring devices built by some star-crazy king. We climbed around the huge red stones not really understanding how they worked, bought a banana, and strolled around waiting for dinnertime.

Dinner on this 31st Independence Day was supposed to be chicken tandoori, but we had to settle for roast beef, potatoes, and lots of cold, filtered but probably not-too-healthy water.

After dinner I sat down to TV—it was kind of homey. I saw the news report of the Prime Minister's (Desai) Independence Day speech, the highlights of the Commonwealth Games from Edinburgh, a little documentary about India's "marvelous" train system called "Moving Millions," and the English language news, which was basically a flood report.

At 10:00 we went on down to the theater to catch the hottest Indian flick of the season. It was a little entertaining but nowhere near as good as last night's. Once again, "intermission" meant "exit, stage anywhere" to us.

Wednesday, August 16: Delhi

I wasn't looking forward to today. I knew we'd have hassles, and in the back of my mind I expected it to take most of the day, but the bureaucratic merry-go-round we rode today to get our plane tickets to London was insane. I even dread going through it again for the sake of this journal.

We started off by checking several airlines just to be sure we weren't missing any spectacular deals—we weren't. I did stand in a 30-minute Aeroflot line just to find out that the Russians don't even sell tickets in India. Confident that we had the best deal possible, we scootered back to the Student Travel Agency at the Imperial Hotel and booked onto the September 5th 00:55 flight from Delhi to London for $335. They couldn't confirm us until September 1st, they said, and I became kind of a pain in their ass wanting assurance that we wouldn't miss our charter home. To get the ticket at this price, we had to change the full charter price of the ticket ($435) at a special bank and then, because it was a student travel bureau, they would refund us $100 or 800 rupees, which is virtually all of their commission. I got the jitters though when their "man" led us to a dumpy little "bank" on the third floor of a slummy building in a sleezy looking office room. Several lost-looking tourists, who also wanted flights back to Europe, were sitting in the waiting room and I asked, a bit defensively, why we were taken to this bank. The guy said we could go to another if we liked. I didn't feel comfortable changing $880 here, so Gene and I took off to think things over and check things out.

We took a three-wheeler to Thai Airways and they said the student office was reliable. We went to a big bank and with a reasonable line. So, after picking up mail at American Express, we found ourselves back in the dingy little waiting room—waiting for them to take our $880. I sat there enjoying all the letters I got from my family & friends. Everyone came through with very enjoyable letters and the long wait didn't bother me a bit. Then we signed over our traveler's checks and returned to the student office. We were told to come back at 5:00 and we spent the rest of the afternoon in banks, airline offices, bumping around Delhi in one-rupee scooter rickshaw rides, and buying a great canvas suitcase-like bag to put all the junk we'll be flying home with.

At 5:00, as I stepped in, a happy man who I thought hated me by now greeted me with, "Good news, you're confirmed to London!" Wow, was I relieved. I have a hunch he just put it down "confirmed" to shut me up, but it says OK on my Delhi-London ticket, and if, in September, it's not, I have grounds to really raise hell. Now we bought all-day tours of Delhi for tomorrow and $20 Royal Nepalese flights from Kathmandu to Patna for August 26th. Wow—everything was done and all we wanted to do was collapse in our quiet room and stare at the hypnotic ceiling fan. We did.

After a shower, a dinner, and a couple hours of very amateurish Indian TV climaxing with a high-school-ish Calcutta music concert (Western music just doesn't belong in India), I caught up on the journal and went to bed.

Thursday, August 17: Delhi

Breakfast was fortified with super zinc vitamins and our weekly malaria pills (they must be working great because neither of us has malaria yet). We took a scooter to the Imperial Hotel and waited to catch our all-day, 8-rupees Delhi tour. Today was to be the day that we really made up for lost time and finally saw the town. We waited and waited to catch our 9:30 tour.

Shortly after 10:00 we boarded the bus full of Indian tourists and for the next half hour we wandered around picking up more passengers. I figured this would be a hopeless waste of time but at 10:30 we hit the road and the next seven hours were great as we busily clicked off the sights of New and Old Delhi.

First, we drove south out of town to the Qutub Minar, a tall, impressive tower and the first mosque in India built around a mysterious iron pillar. Just as our guide told us we would have 30 minutes to see the place, the monsoon ripped loose and we had no choice but to get drenched. That's ok though—it's so hot and sweaty I'd almost prefer to be like stepping out of a shower with my clothes on.

After a short stop to check out some "Cottage Industries," we drove on to Humayun's Tomb. This tomb predated Shah Jahan's Taj Mahal and kind of inspired it. It's evident that the architect of the more famous Taj had the beautiful Humayun's Tomb in mind. It's a pity the weather was so dreary because photography could have been outstanding.

After a quick run through the governmental center seeing India Gate, National Ministries, the Parliament, and the Presidential Palace—all built by the British but finding their place in the current Indian government—we stopped at the Lakshmi Narayan Temple.

This was my first real major Hindu temple, and I really was fascinated by it. (I love note-worthy firsts on the road.) Barefoot through the puddles I wandered, soaking in uncountable statuettes, paintings, mini shrines, pilgrims, verses, and lessons written in English as well as Hindi, and music. The architecture was unique, like nothing I'd ever seen before, and the gods and goddesses were eerily captivating. At the entrance, accompanied by a rag-tag band of temple musicians, several people gathered to pray.

That temple was great. I could have stayed longer but, rushed, I put my shoes back on and caught our tour bus. Now it was lunch time and we stopped at a greasy restaurant of very questionable sanitation, and I shouldn't have had the fish and rice. Feeling lousy, I found a secluded garden to take a pee in, savored a few glucose biscuits, and once again our tour was underway.

Now we left New Delhi for Old Delhi and our first stop was the impressive little Gandhi Museum where I spent 30 very educational minutes learning

My first real major Hindu temple,
Lakshmi Narayan Temple.

about that great Indian leader. After short visits to memorials of India's three greatest modern leaders, we made our last stop for the day—the Red Fort.

Built by the Mughal rulers, descendants of Genghis Khan, this was a huge, strong, and of course, red fort. Inside, the mosques, palaces, and Mughal Museum were all good to see and by 5:00 we were back in the center of Delhi and taking a scooter home.

Now suddenly, I felt worse than I had at any other time in 80 days of traveling. I've been so lucky for so long health-wise, and I figured now it was my turn. With a miserable stomach, kind of constipated, and even with a fever, all I wanted to do was lie under the fan. We planned to go to an evening of Indian dance and music, but I could barely take my shoes off. I wanted to see this performance very badly and after 15 minutes' rest I put on my long pants and "dress" t-shirt and gave it a try. We caught a scooter and in 10 minutes I was inside the cool, modern, rich Oberoi Intercontinental Hotel. Just the coolness of the air and the classy atmosphere made me prefer this to our hot room, and I was feeling much better.

Just then there was a power outage and I thought it was kind of nice that even the luxurious Oberoi has to light up the stubby little emergency candles when Delhi has electrical problems.

We took the elevator to the ninth floor hoping the electricity would stay on, and after a great view of Delhi spreading under the hazy setting sun, we paid 20

Left: The Gandhi Museum proved enlightening during our tour of Delhi.
Right: The Lahore Gate, entrance to the expansive Red Fort.

rupees ($2.50) each and sat down in the front row, psyched for some Indian folk music and dance.

The tabla, harmonium, flute, and sitar started happily in and then we were treated to six or eight lovely Indian folk dances from all different regions of India. I always thought Indian dance was somber and serious, but these were gay, goofy, and spirited, kind of like American folk dances. The dancers and musicians were having a good time, getting into it, and I think having a few private jokes on the very touristy audience. I really enjoyed it—I felt pretty good an hour and a half later when we walked out. I also admitted to myself that, someday, I would like to be able to travel in this first-class style; taxis instead of scooters, screwdrivers instead of "Limca" (the local 7-Up), air-conditioning instead of fans, and Intercontinentals instead of YMCAs. But, as that dream requires dollars instead of cents, and a successful businessman instead of the income of a piano teacher, I steered myself away from those fantasies and back into my humble economic reality. Or perhaps more economic power just happens as you age past 23.

After a browse through the bookstore and a scooter ride home, we paid our 340-rupees bill for our four nights here and packed up for tomorrow's journey. I bought a cute cheapy canvas suitcase at the super bazaar and everything we wouldn't need for the next two weeks we put in there and checked at the YMCA. That left us with wonderfully light and little packs to carry on to tomorrow's flight to Gorakhpur.

Ready to go, we ordered our wake-up call for 4:45, to be followed by 5:00 breakfast, to be followed by a taxi ride, to be followed by a 6:45 flight east, and went to bed early.

Friday, Aug 18th.   Delhi - Tansen, Nepal

As planned we were woken at 4:45, breakfast
came at 5:00 + by 5:30 we were on the road. We
decided to skip the [...] take the [...] taxi
ride to the a[...] [...] + faster
+ just a li[...]
   The air[...] a quick
fresh + ba[...] my
knife we [...] [...]. The
propellers tur[...] + we let
New Delhi. R[...] beautiful
Indian stewardess [...] during she broug
by. After breakfast she [...] me fresh squeezed man
juice — Oh what lovely mangos! After 90 minutes we
landed in Kanpur, lost a few + gained a few passeng
and we sped down the wet runway. The landing gear
disappeared into the wing outside of our window + we
above a flooded India. I've looked at a map before
wondered why India has no lakes but now I see that
during the monsoon season, half of India is a lake. T
countryside was so lush + green + thriving in the lif
waters of [...] I survived a trip to the
plan[...] airborne
[...] hope

CHAPTER 8

Everyone Smiled—
Pokhara, Nepal

August 18–21

Friday, August 18: Delhi to Tansen, Nepal

As planned, we were woken at 4:45, breakfast came at 5:00, and by 5:30 we were on the road. We decided to skip the airport bus and take the $3 taxi ride to the airport which would be faster, more reliable, and just a little more expensive.

The airport experience was smooth, and after a quick frisk and bag check and a warning not to take out my knife, we boarded our Dutch-made Fokker plane. The propellers turned over like they have for decades and we left New Delhi. Right away I was struck by the beautiful Indian stewardess. I took two of everything she offered. After breakfast she gave me fresh squeezed mango juice—oh what lovely mangos!

After 90 minutes we landed in Kanpur, lost a few and gained a few passengers, and we sped down the wet runway. The landing gear disappeared into the wing outside of our window and we rose above a flooded India. I've looked at a map before and wondered why India has no lakes, but now I see that during the monsoon season, half of India is a lake. The countryside was so lush and green and thriving in the life-giving waters of the rainy season. I survived a trip to the plane's bathroom. Going down the aisle was like walking on a trampoline and using it was like sitting in an airborne outhouse. I enjoyed a view of the rain-soaked Indian countryside through the hole below (another first for me). I hope I don't get lockjaw from the rusty lid. Back in my seat, the stewardess with the red-dotted forehead and the powerful smile sari-d down the aisle handing out sweets and freshies. What a lovely alternative to surface travel! This is a new experience for me—having air travel as an economically feasible alternative to surface travel. This three-hour flight cost $27. Our wheels hit Gorakhpur with a splash, and we stepped out of our Calcutta-bound plane into a wicked rain, finding ourselves in a very strange wilderness landing strip.

Around us was dripping jungle. It looked as if it had been raining nonstop for a hundred years. The plane sat on a strip of runway as wide as a two-lane street. An ancient plane was rusting and overgrown next to the trees nearby, and an old car was waiting to shuttle us away. The regular bus wasn't working so we piled into a big, 1950s-vintage American car and drove to the airport waiting room. It was more like a sheltered bus stop than an airport but at least it offered shelter from the relentless downpour. I was kind of enjoying this monsoon-India. It's so warm that the wetness is just wetness and this is undeniably a big part of life in India. The deluge wettens the collective smile of this land. These people live with this, happily, for a good chunk of every year. Water is life.

We took a scooter through swamped Gorakhpur, laughing at our crazy situation. We were stuffed into this tiny three-wheeled scooter, forcibly reclined in the broken back seat with two other people, rain drooling all over the place, and the driver's pink plastic tarp flapping in our faces doing more to sprinkle water than to shield us from it.

We got to the bus station at 10:45 and asked when the next bus to the Nepal border was. 10:30 was the answer. The 10:30 bus is that in name only. It goes only after it comes and it comes sometime after 10:30.

Now it struck me—I was deep in India. Delhi seemed like India after Kashmir but it was so Western and tame. Here I was in a car-port-like bus station and there was no English script anywhere—not even our numbers. Everything was in totally foreign Hindi. People squatted around in groups, painted, draped, wet, and not caring. Buses routinely came late; time has no value. You have to spend 24 hours somehow to live a day and this way was as good as any. Then two guys in white robes walked in with long vicious spears! Wow! I had to go over and check that out! Spears!

We joined some other travelers in renting a jeep to go to the border. For 10 rupees each, a guy would take his Bombay-made Jeep with seven people packed into it on the two-hour ride. That's a cheap Jeep, and we climbed in. I sat in front with the driver and my Indian friend, and Gene had to pack into the back with five others. We weren't tourists anymore—there are no tourists around here, only travelers. With drips dropping everywhere and puddles exploding out from under the Jeep, we headed north, hoping the roads were still navigable.

What a ride. I was in the highest of spirits as we zig-zagged madly through the holy cows, drenched passing bicyclists, and bounced to the rhythm of the blaring Indian movie music as everyone on board sang along. I couldn't tell if the bodies of water that stretched sometimes for miles on either side of the road were lakes or floods. I suspect these "lakes" were seasonal. After a tea stop and lots of glucose biscuits we came to the border.

The India-Nepal border was, as might be expected, a strange border. The Indian office was a desk in a tea shop with a laid-back, friendly bureaucrat who slowly and routinely stamped passports. We met a Peace Corps volunteer who had served two years in Nepal there, and he was fascinating to talk to. That guy had really experienced Nepal and he had grown to love the country, its mountains, its wilderness, its tempo of life, and especially its people. He was happy to be leaving India and returning to Nepal.

When I asked him about health, he was nonchalant, "Oh, I've been pretty good really. I haven't had dysentery for quite a while and the Peace Corps fixes us up fine with vaccinations. I've got worms though." (They say along this Hippie Trail to Kathmandu there are two kinds of travelers: "those who know they have worms and those who don't.")

Worms. Well—I guess I'll be careful while I'm here and drag any worms out before they get all the way in. This morning Gene and I took the first of our supposedly "miracle pills." Brand new, and at a dollar a piece, they should be miracle pills in protecting us from any miscellaneous bugs that knock on our door.

Under the happy "Welcome to Nepal" arch and through the puddles we walked. Ooo, I was thrilled to be here, and I was glad to be coming over land and not flying into Kathmandu. There's something particularly right about crossing a country overland rather than flying effortlessly into its major city.

Right away I knew this place was different. It was special. It was Nepal. Everyone smiled and had a sense of humor—rickshaw bikers, customs officials, and little poor kids splashing playfully in the mud. This was one of the poorest

Reaching Nepal, the "Kingdom in the Himalayas," was like arriving at the summit of our journey.

countries in the world, with a per capita income of just over $100 a year. This is a country that India gives aid to. This is a place that makes India look advanced. But this is a proud, peaceful, happy, and as far as I can tell, content land. I'm so glad to be in Nepal.

The Nepali customs were a breeze. We got 1,195 rupees for $50 and got used to the Nepali rupee worth eight cents instead of the 12-cent Indian rupee. I expect things will cost the same amount of rupees here, meaning only 2/3 as much as in India. Piling onto a minibus, we rode for four cents into Bhairahawa, the first town across the border.

What an eye-opening ride! I clung to a corner of a bench and just gawked at the people around me. There was a great change. The Nepalis looked more Tibetan or Mongolian. The lady in front of me was beautifully adorned—deep

Nepal is so poor, India gives it aid. And a water pump is a gift that gives and gives.

blue-and-red sari, a large brass ring shining from her nose, tattooed hands, and seven holes in each ear. I counted them myself. She had four gold earrings and three empty holes including one large see-through model. The bracelets covering her forearm and the healthy twinkle in her eyes made her quite an impressive sight. Unlike my impression of Indian women, she was independent and in control enough to look me right in the eye. For lack of an alternative form of communication, she smiled. Across from her, an old man carefully fingered a pile of money in his hand that couldn't have amounted to more than 5 cents. Then, next to me, a fat girl wrapped in red silk leaned over her smiling husband and wretched out the window, making a very miserable face and then regaining her composure as if nothing happened. Worms…

We got to a crossroads lined with woven roofed shelters and pineapple and coconut salesmen. This was Bhairahawa and we stepped out. After being warmly received at the new raggedy tourist information booth (I think we made the underworked attendant's day), we found out that buses would run until 4:00 and a good plan was to head for Tansen tonight and carry on to Pokhara tomorrow.

We boarded a bus to Butwal—the last town on the Indian plain—butted right up against the Himalayan wall. This was a friendly bus. Buddhists, curious women, happy fat men, and four goats—three black and one white. I shared my front bench with the shaved Buddhist and the three black goats. I struck up a conversation with a delightful man who had served in the British army but liked the quiet Nepal countryside better. He warmed me all over just by talking with me. He said he couldn't visit me in America but he would see me in paradise.

With a heartfelt handshake and a great belly laugh, he stepped off the bus and out of my life—forever. (I'm learning the world is filled with such people.) I offered my treasured glucose biscuits to everyone around me and, predictably, no one accepted. (To be honest, that was both my hope and expectation.) Gene and I munched as we approached Butwal and the exciting first hills of the Himalayas that vanished into the heavy monsoon clouds.

Butwal was exciting. Not much really, but this was Nepal and being in a new culture, simple things take on a fresh appeal. Boys balancing baskets of chickens on a pole, the new brands of bottled soft drinks of questionable cleanliness, a strange mix of local clothing with loud bell bottoms and Western t-shirts, men sitting tightly cross-legged under the shelter of their bicycle rickshaws, and pigs rolling in the sputtering-on-the-rain mud. A frog dashed in front of me as we ran to our bus, just catching it as it pulled out. Taking our seats, we were joined by the same four goats, and we rolled out of Butwal. (I love that name—it's so fitting.) Quickly becoming lost in the heavily vegetated mountains, we rose high above the plain.

I was glad we took the slow local bus now and didn't wait for the Pokhara express in the morning. I couldn't imagine a better "welcome to Nepal" tourist activity than enjoying this ride. Everything was perfect. I hung my head out the window and drank in the lush green, charging cliffs, swollen rivers, dreamy waterfalls, green-carpeted terraces, and tropical-looking villages complete with bright-eyed mothers running out with their babies and pointing to the for-

Exploring small-town and village Nepal was a non-stop delight.

eigner who was passing through. Long, frail, suspension footbridges stretched across gorges, and Gene and I were tickled as could be. Suddenly, Gene grimaced in pain. I didn't know what was happening until he said, "That goat is stepping on my foot!"

We climbed for about an hour, and just as darkness set in, we came to lovely Tansen, right on the top of a ridge and a great halfway stop on the road to Pokhara. We were relieved to find it had electricity, and it hit us—this was the first time that the existence of electricity has ever been a concern— we have really escaped it all.

This place was great—totally unspoiled and I can hardly wait to see it in the morning light. Stepping over the goats, we got out and found a nice hotel right on the main square for 16 rupees for the double. It was surprisingly nice with screens on the windows, a clean-looking restaurant, and even canopied beds. The restaurant looked clean, so for 80 cents each, we had chicken, rice, and vegetables with tea. I was writing away in this journal, nearly finished with today's long entry, when Gene came running in excited about a religious ceremony in the streets.

We ran through the dark alleys and caught up with the mysterious parade: 20 young men in dress-up white outfits and four with green leis or necklaces were holding hands and singing the same song over and over, moving slowly down the street surrounded by half of the village, drawing people to every window and illuminated by six men wearing kerosene lanterns like hats. Two very sparkling and painted women, looking like princesses or goddesses, followed silently under a brightly colored umbrella, and behind everyone were the drummer and harmonium player with their men carrying their instruments with straps across their foreheads. Making a commotion in the background was the town fool, very drunk and obnoxious, and a few brawling dogs. We found out that this procession—which would go on for a few hours—was the first anniversary of a Tansen man's death.

It was late and we had to get up at 5:00. We wandered back through a deserted village floating in a wonder-world. The full moon lit the endlessly layered valley and between each row of hills, a white pillow of clouds cuddled. This is Nepal…fully meeting our high expectations.

Saturday, August 19: Tansen to Pokhara, Nepal

Our hotel didn't wake us up but the roosters did. At 4:45 we were up. I surveyed my body: no bugs or Nepali leeches were found! We ordered eight little Nepali eggs boiled and said we'd be back in ten minutes, after a quick run through the town to see what we saw last night by lantern light but today by sunlight. Most of the town was awake and heading for the Buddhist Temple. We peeked in. The same old music was droning away. The bus was leaving for Pokhara in a few minutes, so we crammed down our eggs, saving biscuits, pills, and Tang for the bus, and after a picture of our hotel's sign saying, "For homely. Please get here," we checked out.

Running, we just hopped into the early bus. It was 6:00 and it was pulling out. This was a local bus but quite alright. Plenty of room, only very fast stops and costing about $1.25 each for the six-hour, 120-kilometer ride. The bus went 12 miles or 20 km every hour and we would pull into Pokhara at exactly noon.

From Tansen we wound through the lush mountains, braving rockslides and nearly washed-out roads. At one point, one guy got out and ran down the one-lane "highway," tossing fallen stones out of the way. As our rusty old bus clung to the tenuous edge, I hung my head out the window, looking straight down at a vigorous river, long and lonely rope footbridges, thatched huts, and green, dripping terraces. My spirit soared as we climbed deeper into the ancient kingdom of Nepal. We passed through several small towns and villages. Most were no more than a row of huts along the roadside. Until recently, Pokhara, Nepal's second largest town, was accessible only by air or trail. This road and the one to Kathmandu, 200 km to the east, really opened up this region. Western t-shirts and Eveready batteries had found their way in, but I don't think a lot has changed here. The villagers still squat, wide-eyed, as the buses pass through. I didn't see a single other Westerner from the India-Nepal border to Pokhara.

(This ride reminded me of a book I enjoyed last year at the UW: *Reflections on the Basic Causes of Human Misery*. It made the case that some of the happiest people were happy because they lived on land poor in natural resources and difficult to live on…land that no other group of people wanted. Perhaps this is why the Nepali expression, when at rest, seems to be a gentle smile.)

The kilometers passed slowly as we neared Pokhara and blue sky began beating the clouds away. As we entered the beautiful Pokhara Valley, the bus became very crowded…painfully crowded. For the last 30 minutes a powerful Nepali woman had wedged herself so strongly onto my bench I was nearly hanging from the window. Just as my body started to scream, we pulled into the place they call the bus station. Staggering out, I found myself in another one of those Asian cities that are missing a skyline. Since land is so plentiful, they just sprawl everywhere. Our first task was to set up in a hotel. In a far-out place like this you seek out the tourist area (in Europe, you try to avoid it) and we began walking to the Phewa Lake where the hotels clustered.

Distances were greater than we thought and we walked and walked. We came to a bike-rental place and each got a good set of wheels for three days for $1.80. Now, with much better mobility, we made our way speedily to the scenic lake, passed the king's palace, and came to Pokhara's "freak street." It seems each city along the Hippie Trail from Istanbul to Kathmandu has its "freak street," the place where the hip-set of long-term young, very "on the cheap" travelers hang out, wear local clothes and jewelry, smoke a lot of dope, and really don't worry about passing time. I must be getting soft in my old age because all the cheap hotels along here (50 cents a night) turned me off and we searched on for something a bit more comfortable. On our Middle Eastern adventure two years ago, Ruth and I slept in lots of places that made these look like Hiltons but I guess money corrupts and softens, and I've got more of it now than in 1976. The problem in Pokhara is that all the hotels are either under $2 or over $10 for a double. We just needed order and cleanliness, something around $4 or $5, and simple. We found the Hotel Mount Annapurna.

This was posh, among the top two or three hotels in Pokhara, and we were impressed. Leaving our bikes outside, we were shown a great corner room right on the mountain side, with everything just right, including a private solid-stone bath and Western toilet with a view of the Himalayas that would make you crap your pants! The price was $13 but since this was their off season, he agreed to $10 if we stayed two nights. Gene hesitated but I thought back on all the alternatives and knew that for $5 each this was great. I took it and five minutes later Gene thanked me for the pressure. This was great!

We kicked off our shoes, turned on the fan, and plopped on the beds, hoping the clouds would reveal the mountains they'd been hiding ever since our arrival in Nepal. We were ready for a good lunch.

The dining room was decorated Tibetan and we had chicken chow mein and sweet-n-sour pork for a buck each. The service and setting was royal, the food safe and good, and I knew I would enjoy Pokhara. As I sit here at my desk, barefoot and not even worrying about bugs, I am convinced that the more far away and exciting the place you're visiting, the more value there is in having a nice hotel. In Europe, I'm just fine in a ratty little hovel but here it's so nice to have a refuge. With a comfy refuge, you can step out and into any scene with a good and confident feeling.

We still had three good hours of daylight and I am determined to use every bit of the limited time I have in Nepal to its fullest. We set out on our bikes.

After a sunny, ten-minute ride we came to Devin's Falls, a tiny gorge with a hole to nowhere that a gushing river thunders through and into. The mist and the rainbow watched as the once-peaceful river twisted violently and plummeted out of sight. I didn't know a raging river could just suddenly disappear into the earth like that.

On the roadside, the Tibetan refugee craftsmen were waiting with their fascinating goods spread out before them. I couldn't resist checking this stuff out. Before I leave this place, I think I'll go crazy with a Tibetan shopping spree. They were asking pretty good prices but their handicrafts were so exotic: pounded metal mugs, Buddhist prayer wheels, yak carpets, Chinese cutlery sets (knife and chopsticks) to be hung at your waist, and bells with ethereal resonance. I didn't know enough about the market options yet so we unlocked our bikes and pedaled on to the Tibetan refugee camp.

Here we were greeted with happy cries, and people came rushing from all corners to sell us their stuff. One lady, with a smiley mouth full of gold and a baby hanging onto her saggy breast, held out all kinds of silver bracelets and

---

Left: This man—a virtual human variety store—has little more than an umbrella for overhead. Top: Exploring on a good set of wheels. Bottom: Many Tibetans, fleeing China, work in refugee camps.

rings. It was a delightful scene and I really liked the bright and happy people who gathered around me. After a lot of hard bargaining, I came away with a great silver bracelet and Tibetan ring for 25 rupees. With a goodbye that was echoed 20 or 30 times, Gene and I pedaled down the grassy road back to the main drag.

With the sun low, our spirits high, and our legs tired, we pedaled on to Phewa Lake to see it as the sun sank. That lake blesses this valley. What is a valley without a lake? Nepalis fished, tourists paddled dugout canoes around the lake and, at the little island-like temple sticking out on a peninsula, the hip tourists who inhabit these parts for months at a time lazed under mothering trees, strumming guitars and each other's hair and, of course, smoked the local hashish or ganja.

Smoking hash is cheap and easy here and enjoying it seems almost like a tourist cliché, like drinking beer in Germany or tea and scones in England. In the shadow of Buddha's temple, ten long-haired freaks sat wearing a towel or sun-bleached underwear, staring out over the lake, a white trail of smoke rising above them to the tune of a bluesy harmonica. We bought a pineapple, a melon, a lemon, and a couple grams of hash (all for around a dollar) and returned to our hotel. The valet parked and locked our bikes for us and we went upstairs, got out the pipe, and made a fruit salad to be remembered.

After a great shower, we went downstairs for a funny dinner. I was really living. It was almost silly to consider the prices on the menu—everything was very cheap. After a nice dinner, we went up on the rooftop to survey the moon-lit town of Pokhara and sense as much as we could. Drums and singing, loud crickets, sailing clouds, and I knew the invisible mountains lurked powerfully in the background. It was sense-you-us.

We went to bed early, hoping for a good, clear sunrise.

Sunday, August 20: Pokhara

The monsoon thunder, lightning, and wild rain woke us at 4:30 and we knew there'd be no sunrise on the mountains at 5:30. So we slept until 8.

I had a great breakfast with real and plentiful coffee, and we were ready to go. By now the weather had cleared and, while those clouds still clung persistently to the mountains, we were in for a hot and sunny day.

Pedaling out of our great hotel, we stopped by the funny little "airport" across the street. They fly three daily $10 flights to Kathmandu, with 19 passengers each. We luckily got the last two seats for the 9:30 a.m. flight tomorrow. Noticing that we were getting low on money, we dropped by the bank that looked more like a lemonade stand and cashed $70 more.

Basic Nepali

Rāmrō = good	*Cha = is*
Ṭhika = OK	*Pānī = water*
Namaste = greetings	*Bīsa = 20*
Sastō = cheaper	*Tīsa = 30*
Kēṭī = girl	*Saya = 100*

Now we pedaled "downtown" for our first look at the central business district of this town. The shops were fantastic. We parked our bikes and just strolled around. What an enjoyable little place. I think I am in one of the world's most beautiful corners. People, chickens, cows, water buffalo, and dogs filled the street and there wasn't another tourist to be found. I went a little wild in the shops. My rate of consumption is directly correlated to my mood and I was in a buying mood. Gene and I discovered some great 1979 Buddhist and Hindu calendars with wild pictures on them and gobbled up 20 for gifts. Up the street, I fancied a rustic teapot and asked, "Kati paisa?" (How much money?) The guy weighed it and told me 15 rupees. I got it, four metal cups, and two primitive wooden combs for 25 rupees ($2). I'm starting to think about outfitting an apartment when I get home—it's fun.

I said, "dhan'yavāda" (thank you) and namaste (aloha), making the traditional prayer sign with my hands, and left to explore farther down this street. I wanted to get one of the silly Nepali hats that all the men wear. It looks so cheap and "Wigwam-ish," with orange, red, and blue and the shape of a tea cozy. Gene said it looked like an "Archie and Jughead" hat but the Nepali girls who gathered around thought it looked cute...I like to think that's why they were laughing. I finally found one big enough and paid 15 rupees for it.

We took an interesting walk down a long side street and, with zoom lens poised, I found lots of great shots. The people here are like none other—just plain friendly. I have worked on the language more than I usually do and it's so fun to say the words I know and surprise the people. My vocabulary is growing and I find Nepali easy to remember.

We bought two very cold bottles of the local pop and crossed a threshold with our first sip. That broke the ice, and we gave up on our self-imposed rule of not drinking locally bottled drinks. Basically, though, we tried to reserve our meals for our very clean hotel restaurant. We snacked on the pop and glucose biscuits and called that lunch as we pedaled off through the town to the area north of Pokhara. The biking was hard work but we were well rewarded. Pokhara is blessed with giant peepal trees surrounded by concrete benches and it's a great, cool place for people to sit and "take a rest" like the sign on the tree says. Even the airstrip used what I mistakenly thought was called a "people tree" as its waiting room.

Finally, we came to the end of the road and to the cave. A talkative man with a big flashlight took us hundreds of feet deep into the cool, dark, and dripping cave for a nice little tour. Pedaling back toward town, I got a push up a hill from a little kid on his bike and we coasted past a peopled peepal tree, eventually stopping at a grassy cliff with a commanding view. With mountains stretching across the gorgeous Seti River winding below us we savored the moment. We just sat on the edge watching water buffalo ford the river and both thinking about where we were, from a "step back and be thankful" perspective. Then we realized in our quietude that we were both quite sunburned and we headed home.

Going home was mostly downhill but the intense sun beat on my beaming arms and hands, and there was no shelter to be found. Racing by all the smiling Nepali faces and little children that chased our bikes like dogs, we stopped once for cold drinks. I just had to get a picture of me wearing my funny little Nepali "toppitopi" (hat), guzzling a bottle of pop, under the store's "Go gay with cold drinks" sign.

Not a moment too soon we got home and my arms were really cookin'. The cold shower we wanted came in only hot, which was awful. After letting it run for five minutes, it got cool and so did I. Just to lie under the whirling fan naked and dripping wet felt so good. We did a lot of biking and exploring today.

My beloved mink, Herr Rat, suffered in the hot Delhi climate and became moist and smelly. I took him along to Nepal for dry therapy and every day I whip him around under the fan. Today he's much better: smelling less and getting some of that old Herr Rat gleam back in his hair.

After a cooling-off rest period, we pushed our weary legs out once more to go back to the Tibetan refugee camp. We wanted to shop but, very strangely, no one wanted to sell. That left us just wandering awkwardly around the camp. On the way home, we visited Pokhara's bread factory—wonderfully primitive mass production—and bought four big rolls. They were very hot, just out of the oven, and painted with melted butter.

We were back in our room just in time for the blackout. It was dark and in a few minutes a servant came rushing in with candles and matches for us. Without him, we would have just continued to lie there, content and in darkness, feeling good.

It was about 8:00 when we passed through our flickering hallway and went down for our candlelit dinner. Dinner was so enjoyable. Chicken omelet, rice, sweet-and-sour pork, and lots of good coffee and great Tibetan waiters to talk and joke with. They are really wonderful people and as we learned from them, they learned from us. I explained all the symbolism on the US dollar to them. They taught me to say "beautiful girl": rāmrī kēṭī. I tried to explain to them why some currencies are strong and others are weak but it was difficult. They didn't understand why a rupee wasn't worth a dollar and why a dollar wasn't worth a pound if America is such a powerful country. I then taught them how to make a mushroom out of George Washington. Guiding their fingers, I helped them fold the bill lengthwise twice in a way that hid the lower half of Washington's face so his neck meets his forehead. Creating an American hero named Mushroom Washington brought them great joy and lots of laughter.

Gene and I were both eating well, healthy and happy, and we lingered over a second pot of coffee, just relaxing. It was great to have healthy Gene back.

Monday, August 21, Pokhara

Once again, we woke for the 5:30 sunrise on the staggering mountains and found only clouds. We dozed back off and didn't get out of the hotel until nearly 10:00.

Biking across town, we paused to watch the plane that we'd be on in 24 hours come in from Kathmandu as those awaiting their flight gathered under the peepal tree and the cows on the runway scattered.

We then pedaled back to the Tibetan Refugee camp and did some serious shopping. First, we entered the rug-weaving house and the air was filled by a religious-sounding work chant that all the cross-legged, hard-working women were murmuring. It was strange to see the tedious work mixed up with the circular pattern of the music. Babies, as if calmed by the song, stared out the windows and mothers hammered and wove. Slowly, very slowly, Tibetan carpets of beautiful designs took shape.

In the next building we followed the raw wool down its course, becoming heavy yarn ready to be made into carpet. This wasn't what we came for, though. I wanted to pick up some little gifty stuff. From all corners Tibetans came with their bags of old and new stuff. We sat in the little tea shop and reviewed the wares, showing interest when we wanted to begin a round of bargaining. I got a rugged looking "dragon" bracelet and then decided that I wanted to come away with something substantial that would be a heavy, rustic metal cup or two. Their initial asking price for the cups I liked was 90 rupees each. I offered 100 for the three best cups and that drew laughter—my first offer always does. In the end

I walked away with the second and third best cups for 30 rupees each. Those will be great back in Seattle.

On the road back to town, I met an old guy who looked like he'd been wandering the Tibetan highlands for 60 years. We sat down on the grass and slowly he laid all his merchandise out between us. I didn't see a thing I liked until he carefully unwrapped a Buddhist lama drum. What a curious little drum. I picked it up for 20 rupees and wondered what in the world I would do with it as we rode back to our comfortable hotel.

For some reason I was exhausted and I just collapsed on the bed, noticing how hot my sunburned arms and hands felt. Gene and I shared a chicken omelet and plain rice, and I took a cold shower. I really had a hard time getting back out, but this was our last day here and I wanted to do lots more. Trudging out of the hotel, I trusted my energy would return. And it did.

A Real Dugout Canoe

I have never ridden in a dugout canoe and now was my chance. We biked to Phewa Lake and I had no problem hiring a long, black dugout. Light, fast, and tippy, it was a fun experience…especially after enjoying some Nepali marijuana. Then Gene and I got a more conventional rowboat and clumsily set out to the middle of the lake, where we let her drift while we swam from the boat. This was a fine way to spend the afternoon. I simulated "man overboard" falls and goofed around until we decided to eat our little box of glucose biscuits. Just then clouds hid the sun and, dripping wet, I actually felt cold—a wonderful feeling these days.

We found ourselves drifting to the far side of the lake and into sight came a dreamy little bay lined with old dugouts and rice paddies and bounded by jungle and a waterfall on one side and a village, thatched to a hill on the other side. Wow!

Tropical Waterfalls and Leeches

We would be fools not to check this place out. Our first desire was to climb to that inviting waterfall. We beached our boat, were greeted with namastes by a couple of the local kids, and found the trail that would take us from the beach, through the jungle, and, hopefully, up to the falls.

After 30 or 40 yards we realized this would not be easy. Not only was it more overgrown, the trail was thickly infested with wild and horrifying insects. Some flew and others moved very fast but the one we were shaking about was the nightmarish Nepali leech. Yuck! The thought of some gross, slimy jungle thing sucking my blood was terrible—even rivaling the thought of a hookworm crawling up into my feet, laying eggs, and eventually raising a huge and thriving family in my stomach. Neither of us wanted to trailblaze through the gummy spiderwebs. I didn't think we'd make it to our waterfall until we found a high trail that took us there directly. It was fantastic. The fantasy of a tropical waterfall, it reminded me of an Herbal Essence shampoo commercial.

We just had to shower under the beautiful cascade. Even with the sun behind clouds and the bugs ready to pounce, we stripped to our underwear, climbed out onto the slimy rocks, and lost ourselves in the glimmering, thundering world that totally smashed any other sensation we happened to be entertaining. Under that waterfall, I could feel my smile and nothing else mattered.

After dark, we tended the wounds from our leech wars.

Resting and just hanging around on a dry rock, it came: The Leech… slowly and confidently working its wormy way toward our flesh. I'm sure it could almost taste our blood. Like a heat-seeking slinky, it came slow and steady. Rhythmically, head over tail, it marched as only a leech can toward our pink and uncalloused flesh. We'd stand boldly, luring it toward us and then…at the last moment…we'd take a step away. The leech, undeterred, trudged on. It was strangely thrilling. Finally, we escaped and, while the journey back to the beach was quick, we were always on guard. I was glad leeches don't fly.

On the way, we came upon a long, frantically busy line of ants, really moving along in a fast but orderly single file. I placed a small rock in their path and was fascinated by the confusion that followed, and how a messenger would always be sent back to reestablish communications and set the stupid "follower" ants back on course.

Nice Village — Do These Dogs Have Rabies?

After a restful pause sitting on the rotten hull of a half-sunk, old dugout, and meeting a two-kid welcome committee that came down from the village, we had to venture up there and get a close look at this genuine, unspoiled, virtually untouched village. The crude stone stairway up through the terraced rice paddies was steep, and above us sang a whole chorus of crazy birds. We found ourselves high above the bay, nearly out of hearing range of our waterfall, and looking over at a fairytale cluster of thatched roofs.

We stayed on the outer path until we reached the top of the hill, where we came to something resembling a manger scene. Corn stalks, goats, and cows in a pile of hay, under a thatched roof with a glorious view of Phewa Lake and its Buddhist temple below and, on a clear day, many of the world's highest peaks.

Down the hill a ways, we came to a rather prosperous house with corn cobs drying on the patio, the same view, a dog that was ready to rip me to shreds and, luckily, people. With folded hands we traded namastes and they called off the hound. We were allowed to wander around a bit, but they were not very outgoing hosts.

Further down the hill we followed the path through the rice paddy and came to a very friendly scene. Children were playing and swinging a baby in a hammock under the shade of a heavily thatched eave. An old retired Indian Army man came over and welcomed us. We had a warm conversation and heard about his battles against the Chinese when they invaded in 1962, and against Pakistan in later years. He gets a 290 rupees ($23) a month pension and is living comfortably here in his peaceful village of Anadu.

We said goodbye and made our way down to our boat. When I turned around, there were several people waving goodbye.

We shoved off and, in an extremely relaxed fashion, we half-drifted and half-paddled back past the Buddhist temple to our waiting bikes. It was so wonderful not to have to go anywhere, just to be slow. The boat slowly drifted around, giving me a spectacular, panoramic, 360-degree view of the lake and the Pokhara Valley. I just lay there, letting the current set the tempo and show me the sights on its terms.

Our total bill for 4.5 hours in the boat was about 50 cents. We paid it and pedaled through Freak Street, noticing how aloof we had kept ourselves from that hip group of Westerners and not really caring to intermix with them. We left our bikes at the rental place. They had served us very well and made Pokhara an enjoyable town.

It was dark now as we walked back to our hotel. Once again, there was no electricity, and we were greeted by dancing candlelight and flickering hallways. The dining hall was thriving. We couldn't believe it. We had always eaten totally alone with more than enough servants hanging around to lay the tablecloths on our laps, pour our water, remove bugs that were too big for us to comfortably kill, and do whatever we needed. Now this place was jammed and we actually had to wait for our meal. We enjoyed chicken curry and momos (dumplings) with water buffalo meat. I liked our dining room better empty, but they were happy for the excitement and the big money that was pouring in. We always ordered whatever we wanted, and a full meal never cost more than $2. One trick that widens the experience and cuts the risk involved by 50% is to split all orders and never order the same thing. This way, each night, we got to experiment a bit and enjoy two different entrees in half-portions.

Nothing much went on that night. We went to sleep to the rhythm of a monsoon rainstorm, hoping for—but not expecting—a good sunrise on the mountains in the morning. One of the servants told me he would pray to the gods and goddesses of the sky for good weather in the morning.

CHAPTER 9

Pie, Chai, and Shiva's Ganga—Kathmandu, Nepal

August 22–25

Tuesday, August 22:
Pokhara to Kathmandu, Nepal

We struck out. Three mornings in a row we woke up at 5:30 and never saw the mountains—only clouds, clouds, clouds. We saw the giant mountains but only in bits and pieces, and you don't get the same effect, I'm afraid, by seeing just bits and pieces.

After a shower and the usual breakfast, we packed our bags and said goodbye to all the friends we had made in the Hotel Mount Annapurna and walked across the street to the airstrip. We checked in just before the 30-minute warning whistle went off. That was the signal for the boy to clear the water buffalo off the pasture and get ready for an airplane.

This airport was so cute. I waited under the big peepal tree and watched the arriving plane float across the mountains and zoom by me on the runway. My pack went into a locker in the nose and I climbed into the DHC-6 Twin Otter plane. The interior was great: three seats to a row, one sleepy stewardess who gave us candies, and about 20 people on board for the 30-minute flight to Kathmandu.

The props flipped over and whirled into nothingness. The pilot released something and we jerked into motion, speeding down the grassy runway. Then we were airborne over the thatched huts, lush fields, and tiny water buffalo. In an instant, Phewa Lake was behind us and we were soaring over the lower Himalayas. Below us slept terraced hills, scattered villages, a few brown trails and rivers—and no roads. This was real wilderness. The whole group gawked at the scenery and snapped away on their cameras, until we came over and then into Kathmandu.

Previous page: The temples of Durbar Square mark the center of Kathmandu.
Bottom: Awaiting our plane under the peepal tree at the Pokhara airport.

Kathmandu cityscape

So this was Kathmandu, our ultimate destination. I felt excited, and reaching it, I felt like we had really accomplished something. I was psyched to turn this dream city into reality. This is the ancient capital of the Kingdom of Nepal.

We took a cab to the center of town and I got my first glimpse of the pagoda-style Buddhist and Hindu temples of Kathmandu's Durbar Square. This is what I've always seen in guidebooks and now I'm standing before them.

Before we could enjoy Kathmandu, we had to find a hotel. Nothing good was cheap and nothing cheap was good. We finally gave up and settled for something more cheap than good, but it was located right on the main square. The Sugat Hotel cost 60 rupees for a double with private bath and breakfast. We unpacked and rested for a while, but I couldn't sit still with all those exotic temples just down the street.

I lost myself in Durbar Square. This was a tangled, medieval-ish world of tall, terraced temples; fruit and vegetable stands; thin, wild, and hungry people praying, begging, and going through rituals; children, oblivious to it all, playing tag among the frozen Buddhas; rickshaws; and bread carts. Ten years ago, the only blemishes of our modern world—cars and tourists—weren't there and the sight would have been pure. But even with long, straggly-haired, lacy, baggy-clothed freaks sitting on the stones, and the occasional honking taxi, this was a place where I could linger. It's a living museum, a cultural circus, a story that doesn't need a plot. We put away the guidebook and gave up trying to understand each thing, and just wandered through Buddha's ever-watching, all-knowing eyes, under monkey gods and erotic carvings, and ornately carved temples. Holy men were holy, beggars begged, hawkers hawked, and dwarfs and hunchbacks did their thing.

After a while, we stopped by a thriving little place that was famous in the Hippie Trail lore: Pie & Chai. Joining the hippie crowd, we savored delicious hot apple pie, fresh chocolate banana cake, and milky tea. What a treat.

Now we walked into the more residential section of the city and, after a few good turns, we were deep in the world's only Nepali urban jungle. Before us opened a large square lined by old, fancy, aged-black wooden buildings, full of playing children, many flying frisky little kites. We ducked into a side courtyard and found a neighborhood temple. Actually, it seems all houses had a courtyard formation and all courtyards are a religious temple of some sort. This one was quite fancy. An old man gruffly got rid of all the children, winning us peace to fully appreciate the lovely square. The Nepalis have kind of accepted both Buddhism and Hinduism and I guess their religion is a combination of both. The statues were Buddhas in different forms.

The people here seem to live to be peaceful, kind, and warm. A lot of times their bright eyes and smiles make me smile and I get lots of good feelings. I could spend much more time here.

We had rented bikes for 25 cents a day. We liked the mobility they gave us and we used them to go to the post office and then to the Royal Nepal Airlines office to confirm our flights to Patna back in India. It took forever but we got them confirmed, so we now know that we have 3.5 days to experience the Kathmandu Valley. After a light lunch, we were back at Durbar Square to get some hardcore sightseeing done.

For one rupee we entered the old Royal Palace and were greeted by a toothless, happy old guy, who spoke English with a tiny vocabulary and no concept of grammar. He was fun, if a little difficult to understand, but I did learn a little from him here at the coronation place of the kings and basically the historical/political center of Nepal.

Next, we had a real treat in store. We got to see Kumuri Devi. Known as "the living virgin goddess," she's a young girl without zits or blemishes. When chosen she stays in the special house from the time she's five until she reaches puberty. She leaves only three times a year for religious processions, but she does look over her balcony when the tourists leave some money. She looked down at us with awe-inspiring melancholy in her powerfully painted eyes. I caught her eye and was having a serious stare-down with the world's only living virgin goddess. Hmmm. What an experience!

She vanished and I turned around to find a guy who looked like a devilish King Neptune, with long, greasy, unkempt black hair, a tall cane, only a loincloth covering his bronze body, and a very "apart-from-the-world" look on his face. He was wonderfully framed in an ornate wooden doorway, and the only thing I could possibly do was take a picture.

Now we were hurried, a rare and unpleasant feeling, by an appointment to catch a 4:30 film put on by the Kingdom of Nepal. It was an interesting 20 minutes, showing us parts of Nepal that were beyond the scope of this visit and giving us a valuable insight to some of the customs and local values characteristic of Nepal.

We had about an hour to poke around and we decided to do it by bike. We coasted slowly through this amazing world. We came to a large square, totally away from the tourist center, and climbed the

Temples came with sexy art.

pagoda temple to observe the life and people below us. Some very cute kids followed us around. Then we discovered the temple with erotic art that our guidebooks mentioned. Around the roof of this temple were graphically carved and painted sex scenes. The Nepali kids snickered knowingly as we slowly made our way around the temple, necks craned and mouths hanging open.

We went back home for a short rest and I stepped out on our neat little deck and enjoyed a birds-eye view down on all the market-square-type activity spreading out below me. This hotel is, if nothing else, the best location in town. We're just 50 yards away from that living goddess. Poor thing. After she's released, no man will marry her because as soon as someone makes love with her he will drop dead…or so the story goes. Who wants to risk that? There are really plenty of good-looking Nepali girls around. I have noticed that they don't flirt or even mix with the Nepali men, though.

The folkloric show at the Yak & Yeti hotel came with a particularly endearing smile.

Now it was time to bike over to the deluxe Yak & Yeti Hotel and enjoy an evening of Nepali folk dance and songs. Into the rich hotel district we rode, seeing fancy hotels we didn't even know existed. Then we came to the Yak & Yeti Hotel and the Everest Cultural Society. For 20 rupees we were treated to an evening of colorful and happy dancing.

Ten acts came and went in the fancy mirrored and chandeliered hall. Most were really entertaining. The girls were beautiful and one guy had us cracking up. He would leap on stage with a gleaming smile and dance like he was in ecstasy. Gene and I couldn't help but smile and feel really good as he danced. I think that's what dancing is all about. That was a very enjoyable show.

After the show the rain came down. It didn't look like it would let up, so we rode off into the drenching darkness. I was soaked, my wet hair pasted all over my face, and my jacket not helping a bit. My biggest concern, though, was not getting hit. I couldn't see with my glasses under water but that hardly mattered because the cars and rickshaws were usually without lights. I nearly got clobbered but, ringing the bell hoarse, I made it home. We went over to the Mona Lisa restaurant for a late, light dinner featuring steak we called "tough buff." Water buffalo is so chewy, I couldn't really eat a bite of it…just chew all the goodness out of it and then spit out what remains—gristle that feels like a thick piece of cloth.

After doing a little thinking and dreaming on our balcony overlooking the square filled with strange people, I did a bug check and went to sleep.

Wednesday, August 23rd: Kathmandu

We got an early start and headed for the majestic Swayambhunath Chaitya. The impressive temple on a nearby hill overlooks all of Kathmandu Valley.

Passing through the ever-enchanting Durbar Square, we had to pause to observe the morning activity. So much was happening everywhere: people ringing temple bells, throwing flowers, guys getting shaves on the steps of the temple to Shiva, and old ladies picking lice out of each other's hair. I'm going through my film too fast but around here, it's very hard not to.

We entered Pig Alley and stopped at Pie & Chai for coffee cake, apple pie, and tea, and to listen to Bob Dylan records. An old joker who claimed to be a fortune teller joined us uninvited and started reading my palm and predicting my future. He was so lousy he was entertaining. My lucky day is Friday, my number is seven, and my age is 23. How about that.

Pig Alley is aptly named. We walked among the pigs and the muck, children crapping in the streets, and old people framed in older windows. It was an interesting walk and we passed many colorful worshippers returning from the hilltop temple. After checking out a great temple, we crossed the Bishnumati River on an old pedestrian suspension bridge. Then after walking through a great neighborhood and passing more and more people, and even a small marching band, we came to the base of the hill. Before us was a long stairway lined with Buddhas, beggars, and monkeys! This was a thrill. An old orange-clad holy man gave me bread. I fed the monkeys and we climbed and climbed.

At Kathmandu, the eastern terminus of the Hippie Trail, backpackers gather.

On top we entered a dreamy world. This 2,000-year-old huge stupa and the many surrounding temples were alive, seething with worshippers who climbed this hill to throw rice, light candles, burn things, paste red dots on their foreheads, spin dozens of whirling prayer wheels, murmur and mutter, and worship in other ways that I couldn't understand. So much was happening—a totally sensual experience—the cymbals, flutes, drums, and chanting of the musicians, the sweet smell of flowers and incense, and the constant movement. Above it all stared the all-seeing eyes of Buddha and spoiled monkeys who, like cows, are a religiously favored animal. Gene and I lost ourselves on this busy summit. I wish I understood a bit more about Buddhism and Hinduism.

Before going back down we decided to enjoy the great view of Kathmandu and a box of glucose biscuits. I opened the little box, took out a biscuit and,

like lightning, a rude but effective monkey swiped it right out of my hand! I was startled. He wanted more and, frightened, I timidly tossed him another. I quickly ate one and he came at me, demanding more. I stood up and began to flee but he prowled right after me. A friend joined him and I was about to be viciously double-teamed. Nervously and not wanting to be ripped to ribbons by a holy monkey, I tossed him the entire box and he jumped atop a small temple and, very humanly, ate biscuits one by one intentionally just beyond my reach. I was totally defeated and even slightly wounded, which I will have to treat with iodine. The monkeys may be holy but they're far from clean.

We walked back down and returned to Durbar Square, where we intended to study our info and figure out just what everything is in this very holy maze. I could just sit in this square and observe—I love it. We went from one pagoda temple to the next, climbing a few to check out the views and get a close look at the graphically carved erotic art all around the roofs. Incredible, explicit, and often quite kinky. This "art" was to shock the lightning god and spare the temple from a strike. Really effective, apparently, because all the temples are still standing, never having been struck by lightning. I had to zoom in for a couple of X-rated pictures. After a few more statues and temples, we were ready for a rest back in our hotel (and a cold shower).

We have bikes rented today but so far they've just been sitting there. We decided to ride out to a village called Kirtipur. Coasting out of town, we crossed the river and came first to the impressive university.

This was interesting. Right here, on this campus, was the intelligentsia and the future of a more modern Nepal. Always happy to check out a campus cafeteria while traveling (they offer both cheap food and fascinating conversation), we found it and got in line. There was no choice—we just took what was offered: mutton chow (75 paisa), a crunchy mix of potato chips etc. (50p) and tea (20p). That was so cheap that we ended up getting nine teas, six crunchy mixes, and three muttons, spending only a couple of rupees each. I'm glad I got a glimpse of Nepali campus life. I think if I was Nepali, this is where I'd want to be.

Now we reached the town of Kirtipur. We parked our bikes to a chorus of small voices saying, "I watch bike, me bike watch." We locked them up and climbed the stone stairs into the medieval hilltop town of Kirtipur. I was almost in shock! My mouth hung open as before me was a perfect medieval square—it could have been Germany during the time of Martin Luther. Food and other things draped the buildings, drying in the sun. People washed in the rectangular pond next to the well; the men were gathered under eaves, making music or playing cards; children flew kites or chased wheels with sticks; ornately carved and aged windows framed grandparents and their dog. Yarn was spun while ladies daydreamed. It could have been a Bruegel painting; so much was going on but everything was small and nothing dominated. We namaste-d our way through the long, narrow village, following it up a ridge to the highest spot around. A temple crowned this hill and from here we joined the local people in admiring the pastoral view of Kathmandu Valley, which stretched out before us. I can't remember ever being so content, happy, and at such peace, wonderful peace.

We poked around, walking nearly every street in the town and checking out each medieval courtyard and temple. So much small industry was going on. This town was completely untouched and pure. It's how I wish Europe was.

Gene and I made the long ride back to Kathmandu, returned our bikes, and decided to find a good place for dinner. A town is much more comfortable when you've found a favorite place to enjoy a meal. Up until now Kathmandu has lacked that.

We explored the "New Road" and found the Indora Restaurant on a second floor, overlooking a busy square. This was class: clean, great fans, the high class of Kathmandu's citizens talking over tea, great waiters, and surprisingly cheap food. Happily, we ordered and decided to go easy on our stomachs: fried chicken, cooked vegetables, curd, and tea. We think our stomachs are doing a commendable job of staying healthy and they deserve some praise. With a lavish tip the bill came to $2 each and we returned to the Hotel Sugat.

Now after dark, a special life flourished in Durbar Square. We relaxed out on our balcony and smoked ganja, the smoke of Shiva the Destroyer. This was Nepali marijuana, not hashish, and I believe, as I leaned against the balcony wall, that for the first time I was really high... totally high. This was great— better than hash. All I wanted to do was go out and stroll among the pagodas, flutes,

Marijuana, called ganja in India and Nepal, is sold in the markets like an herb.

and sleeping dogs. I saw things I'd never noticed before. We climbed to the top of a pagoda temple and the temples around us became ducks and dogs. All had those ever-present eyes of Buddha. We got two fat little bananas and had a glorious time trying to peel those buggers. I had a chalky mouth and they tasted terrible. At the foot of one temple some Buddhist monks were jamming.

We took a long walk. Three men sitting around a flame, listening to Indian music (which really came alive for me), discussing the buffer function of Nepal between India and China, and smoking Shiva's ganja, invited us to sit cross-legged with them. They looked like a classical painting as the flames flickered on their golden faces. Later, we climbed to a room full of intense music, cymbals, drums, harmonium, chanters, flutes, and worshippers. What an experience to just sit and observe!

Back in Durbar Square, a cute little beggar girl hung on my fingers and kind of flopped around my body. I liked her until I realized she was just a very accomplished beggar. She dragged me to her house where I decided to excuse myself and find Gene. We went down Pig Alley and gorged ourselves with apple pie, tea, and lovely Rolling Stones music. How I miss my music! The slanted, pie-filled room was full of basically wasted freaks who were kind of doing time in Kathmandu. A Frenchman who looked like Richelieu with long curly hair played chess next to me, and an intellectual-looking guy with John Lennon glasses didn't read his book over in the corner.

We crawled through the forest of Christmas-tree temples and went home. Once again, I proclaimed death to all bugs who had the nerve to land on my bed and carried out the sentence either by squishing or by hot match. After brushing off the bug carcasses, sleep was no problem.

Thursday, August 24: Kathmandu

Not much went right about this morning. It was noon by the time we had eaten breakfast, changed money, and found the trolley to take us to Bhaktapur. I really dislike, even hate, needless waste of time when time is limited—and it nearly always is. Nothing went smoothly and changing money took nearly an hour.

Oh well, we took the long, slow trolley ride to the old town of Bhaktapur, about ten miles from Kathmandu. It was well worth the ride and we spent four interesting hours wandering around.

The narrow streets were broken by courtyards, many with the typical pagoda temples. Every big important town has a Durbar Square and Bhaktapur's was great. This place is a lot quieter than Kathmandu and somehow it seems as if the people are different. Maybe they just don't know what tourism is.

We just poked around the Durbar Square area, climbing the big steps, checking out the sexy carvings, and going through the National Art Gallery. There's a strange mixture of ornate and stark here and the effect is fantastic.

Following our noses, we got ourselves turned around in this fantasy land of green soupy ponds, snotty-nosed kids crying in doorways, straw mats covered

with drying peppers, and lounging cows. Paint-smeared faces appeared on people and stone gods, kids with raggy shirts ran around bottomless—a little boy was peeing in the street and ran after a dog before he was through—and processions of sweating ladies carried huge loads of green grass up the streets, with bands across their foreheads. This was a rich experience and by 3 p.m. we were quite tired and ready for a bite to eat in a great little restaurant right across from the tallest pagoda temple in the valley…the perfect spot for a mutton omelet!

After one last stroll through Bhaktapur's Durbar Square, we were ready to return to Kathmandu. Packing into a minibus, we endured a long, 45-minute, 10-mile ride on a very crowded bench. Across from me, next to a lady with seven rings in each ear, a lady calmed her child by nursing her while singing softly and the ride went on and on.

Back in Kathmandu we took a bicycle rickshaw home and found our room newly carpeted! Wow, that really made the place and we're feeling more and more comfortable there.

We each had good, solid bowel movements, cause for celebration in this part of the world. Gene rested while I went out to do a little exploring. There are a lot of tourists in Kathmandu and just as many locals out for their money. Consequently, the square outside our hotel is lined with 4' x 6' carpets, covered with artificially aged knickknacks, jewelry, knives, pipes, and whatever you like. Past the square, most of the little shops are handicrafts and souvenir stores. If you do find a place without gift shops or carpets on the sidewalk piled with knickknacks, you'll be hit up momentarily by a guy selling knives, hash, or a ride in his rickshaw. Other little kids just stick out their hands and weakly ask, "One rupees please?"

I wasn't really looking for Nepali Army surplus knives but a kid gave me a first price of 60 rupees and I was quite shocked. First prices are close to meaningless. From there, you proceed to fight the price down with the goal of walking away with a bargain. I countered his 60 rupees with 20 and eventually bought the sturdy big knife for 31 rupees, or $2.50. After a little more shopping and seeing nothing I either wanted or could justify buying, the rain began and I went home to show Gene my new knife. Boy, I'm getting a lot of junk!

Now it was dinner time and we decided to be lazy and safe and just went back to our nice, classy Indora Restaurant down on the New Road. We brought iodine so we could drink their water, had a loaf of bread (BYOB), and freely ordered entrees of sweet-and-sour pork (so tasty!), roast chicken, boiled eggs, curried vegetables, and rice. Happily stuffed, we paid $1.50 each and walked home.

It was dark, the square hummed with muffled activity, and we stepped out onto our balcony with a funny-looking cigarette of ganja. After a few watery-eyed, smoky moments we were stepping back into the world of yak, yeti, Kumari, and Shiva.

I doubt if I want to get high very often in the future but it really is an incredible experience. While everything is vividly alive and more intense than normal, nothing seems to be real and that scares me a little. Before I always shunned pot as a token of my self-discipline and control. Now I smoke it as a token of self-control and to widen my view of the world. I never could conceive of philosophers doubting reality or pondering another reality. Now I can see that much more exists than meets the eye (or the straight brain).

Perfectly stoned, we wandered through dark Durbar Square. I think this was a good night: Everything seemed to be happening. In the courtyard of "the living virgin goddess," Kumari, we found a large group of people gathered around a very animated speaker who seemed to talk forever and never slow down. We dropped by a few hours later and he was still going. We hung around for a while, just looking at all the people and hoping that the living goddess would make an appearance. She never came out, so we left. Gingerly, we climbed to the dizzy top of a pagoda temple and found some sleeping locals. This was a good perch to observe the square, and observe we did.

We passed a small group of ganja-ed musicians and headed down Pig Alley to Pie & Chai. Pie & Chai is the kind of shop everyone would like, just down the street. Friendly atmosphere, always there with good music, fresh pie and cake, and plenty of tea. We sat in the corner and went "Pig Alley wild." We each went through three big slices of mostly apple pie and three cups of tea.

Pie & Chai, the cherry on top of the Hippie Trail, gave me some of the best times of my young life. Just imagine—hot apple pie coming out of the medieval brick pizza oven, peacenik/music lover/poet/philosophers from around the world to dream out loud with, the best in classic rock & roll from Creedence to the Doors to Dylan to the Stones, and marijuana that makes you as high as the Himalayas that surround you and corrals it all so nothing spills. I'm not just saying this because I'm high…my Pie & Chai memories are pure happiness.

The music was very special. Either this little shop has the greatest speakers in the world, or I have found a way to step right into the music. When you're high, the music has dimension; not only great separation but it engulfs you. It opens its arms and lets you walk in. You are right there and the littlest musical things that always passed unnoticed now jump right out at you! Wow, what a wonderful key to open up such a sensual wonderland. I will guard that key, take it home, and put it to good use there.

Friday, August 25: Kathmandu

We slept in and I really felt quite lazy. The morning was dull: breakfast, shower, and write a postcard. Later today, we planned to go to Patan but we had a few hours of more or less free time first.

I walked down Freak Street and discovered that clothes were the real bargain in Kathmandu. I went on a bit of a spree and by noon, I had a whole new outfit! I was getting tired of always wearing my shorts and yellow t-shirt. First, I checked through all the shops and then I made the rounds again, bargaining my heart out and walking away with baggy, lightweight drawstring pants for $2, a white "work shirt" ($2), two handwoven wool vests for $6, a little pouch, and three notepads of Nepali rice paper.

It felt good to get that out of my system. I went back to the room, rested, and was happy with my new outfit. I just wonder if I'll like it back in Seattle.

Happy Birthday to Krishna...

Today is Krishna's birthday and we're going out to Patan to celebrate. Lazy, we hired a bicycle rickshaw from our front door and for nearly 30 minutes we enjoyed the passing city while we were pedaled to the next town.

Patan is kind of a special city. More Buddhist than Kathmandu, it used to be an independent country. We found its famous Buddhist monastery and got a good look at the Buddhist style. Prayer wheels, big bells, fiery dragon-type things, flowers, and big, golden serene Buddhas. It all seemed to remind us that China was just over the mountains from here. Next, we toured a lovely five-storied Hindu temple to Shiva and then the mid-afternoon hunger pangs set in.

It's funny, when I'm hungry, all other desires shrink and my mind is set on finding food. The problem was, in Patan there are absolutely no restaurants. There were a few dark dens where people lined up with hastily wiped-off plates to eat something that had been over the fire, with their bare hands, but that wasn't for us. I would have enjoyed the experience (if not the taste) of eating in one of those places, but Nepal is no place to be overly adventurous with food, and maintaining your health should always get first priority. I think Gene and I are two of the only healthy tourists around (well, I guess it's not that bad, but a lot of backpackers do get sick in Nepal) and I want to keep it that way.

So, desperate to eat something in Patan, we found a can of Calcutta-made peanut butter, bought six mini-bananas and a fresh loaf of bread, and realized we had no knife. We walked around, wondering what to do, and found a store that had knives that were too expensive to buy and they wouldn't rent them out. Then I had to resort to good old American ingenuity and we used my dirty old fingernail clippers to spread the oily peanut butter. It wasn't a good picnic but it helped our hunger, and now we were ready to see the Patan Durbar Square, and dive into the crowds of colorfully dressed Hindus who were here for the birthday festivities.

Crowds of people mobbed the Krishna temple and a 200-yard line of women snaked down the street from the temple. There was energy here on this special day and the few wide-eyed tourists were quite enthralled by it all.

The King is Coming!

Then we saw lots of police and Boy Scouts clearing the road and the square, and people were gathering for what looked like a parade. We grabbed a good place and waited. We didn't really know what for, but we waited. Everyone crowded along the road and finally someone told me the King and Queen were coming. King Birendra was a young, pudgy, Harvard-educated monarch, who wore glasses like I had in sixth grade. Basically accepted by all but the college liberals, who were quite trivial in number, his passage was occasion for a crowd, lots of police, and a long wait.

We waited and waited. My camera was set up and ready and it got darker and darker, until I ran out of f-stops and photography became hopeless. After an hour or so, we joined a row of tourists who, for some reason, were allowed special front-row seats and we waited longer. I had a good conversation with a German who was working in good old Butwal. Then the crowd rose to its feet, and with a flashing red-light escort, the king sped by, not even acknowledging the crowd that had waited nearly three hours to get a glimpse of his royal face, and he went into the Krishna temple. He worshipped as the press flashed pictures and, back in his fancy car, he zoomed away. Quite a disappointment. He could have at least waved.

We mingled among the seething crowd that had flooded back into the Krishna temple and then decided that it was time to head back for dinner, since there was surely no dinner to be found in Patan.

A bus came and everyone literally fought to get on. In a gamey mood, I literally dived in and actually got a seat. It reminded me of old Rolling Stones concerts. Nothing like a good fight for the door. Inside it was solid people. Breathing air filtered and warmed through the hairs of 60 Nepali armpits, we could see nothing but sweaty bodies. It took a while, but this 2-cent bus ride finally got us back to Kathmandu and, after a short bicycle-rickshaw ride, we were back at Hotel Sugat, and ready for dinner.

All across the Hippie Trail, the backpacker on a tight budget had a challenge with each border: to spend all of his money without running out. This took some planning but was quite fun. And it was time to play that game again as tomorrow we fly to India. For our third night in a row, we went to the Indora for dinner. But this time they let us down. Gene got only three French fries with his chicken and all my "pork" in the sweet-and-sour mix was fat. We called this to the waiter's attention and the situation was rectified.

Quite full, we went home to pack. Getting everything I had picked up into my rucksack became a challenge and I had to work at it.

I wanted one last walk through old Kathmandu alone. I slowly soaked it all in one more time. The silence in the shadows of timeless pagodas. The trancelike music of the ganja-passing musicians, with people gathered by the pull of the ringing cymbals. Dark, muddy streets with shadow dogs lurking and silent ponds. Stone lions in pairs coming to life with each passing headlight and, of course, one last tea and apple pie down at Pie & Chai, with all the wasted freaks. I concentrated on my pie and the music, while playing a mute, half-hearted game of chess across from a German girl. I traded queens, paid my 3 rupees, and stepped back into the streets.

The candle still made Buddha glimmer and shine on the ground floor of our hotel. The desk boy was sleeping when I passed. I went to sleep thinking about our morning flight to India.

Indians and Nepalis are wonderful with signs...

"Hotel for homely, please get here" (Tansen)

"Avoid touching. Keep yourself away" (Varanasi museum)

"Go gay with cold drinks!" (Pokhara)

"Passing of urine not allowed" (Kashmir)

"Corn flex; fried cheaps" (menu in Delhi)

"Life vest your under seat" (Nepali airplane)

Waiting...waiting...waiting for the king.

Saturday, Aug. 26th. Katmandu - Vernasi

I really don't trust my watch. And I don't trust our hotel's wake up service but we managed to get up and out of our hotel _____ after 7:00. A raggy rabble of a _____ _____ jaunt through the _____ _____ to the Hotel Mak _____ we had to blow _____ _____ _____ so we ordered _____ _____ _____ omelet and _____

We met 2 _____ _____ _____ yesterday. They were the _____ _____ we've had the pleasure of meeting in Nepal. The heavy freak scene is kind of depressing & it was fun to talk to those guys.

For 15 is we took a taxi to the airport and found our plane scheduled to leave at 10:15 instead of 9:00. We should have expected this but it took us by surprise. Oh well— that gave me a chance to take care of a couple of post cards & catch up in the old journal. (This thing is really a lot of work)

"Checking in" was interesting. We paid our 40 is each for airport tax and then _____ _____ us to put all our _____ _____ _____ _____ check _____

Saturday, August 26: Kathmandu to Varanasi, India

I really didn't trust my watch. And I didn't trust our hotel's wake-up service, but we managed to get up and out of our hotel by just after 7 a.m. A raggy rabble of a marching band did its morning jaunt through the square and we went down to the Hotel Nakapur for a fancy, last breakfast. We had to blow 30 or 40 rupees before we left so we ordered freely. I enjoyed a cheese omelet and a delightful Nepali hot porridge.

For 15 rupees we took a taxi to the airport and found our plane was now scheduled to leave at 10:15 instead of 9:00. We should have expected this, but it took us by surprise. Oh well, that gave me a chance to take care of a couple of postcards and catch up on my journal (this thing is really a lot of work).

"Checking in" was interesting. We paid our 40 rupees each for airport tax and then they told us to just carry our swollen luggage on. At the baggage check I had to deposit my big Army surplus Gurkha knife, but I passed the frisk and my boarding pass was stamped OK.

After a bit of a wait, we boarded our twin-engine, propeller-driven plane and took off. The 55-minute flight offered good views of Nepal flattening into India, a meager but better-than-nothing box lunch, and a chance to have a Nepali beer. "Star Beer" was nothing special, but it was something I had at least wanted to try.

Before long we had landed in Patna and were waiting to go through Indian Customs. I agreed to carry through a bottle of whiskey and a carton of cigarettes for someone who had bought extras in the duty-free shop. I guess it's easy to get $20 or more for a bottle of liquor in India but I really didn't feel like making money off an Indian alcoholic.

I'll never forget the stoner in front of me in that line. Moments before he was to be checked by the customs man, he discovered a hunk of hashish in his coat pocket. Looking around frantically and not knowing how serious it might be if he was caught with that, he realized there was only one thing he could do at that point. He ate it.

After passing customs, we shared a taxi with some French people and went to the station to catch the Varanasi-bound train. It felt good to be back in India again. A train for Varanasi was leaving in 30 minutes and that was exactly what we needed. First-class tickets were for some reason quite expensive so we decided that this would be our day to weather a six-hour, second-class Indian train ride. The ticket cost about $1.50. We were gluttons for punishment.

On platform 2, we waited for our train, expecting a mob scene when it came. Actually, it wasn't all that bad. We found our way onto a car with all the seats taken but two high beds empty, so we crawled up there and laid claim. We felt like luggage stretched out where in a European train, you'd find peoples' bags.

The next five or six hours were actually enjoyable from our sweaty little roost. Peanut shells were everywhere, some bugs had found my juicy body, every once in a while a very sad-looking beggar would wail by and everyone would totally ignore the poor wretch, and usually two or three men were singing terribly and too loud.

I managed to lose myself in our old but unread Time magazine when I didn't want to feel like I was in a filthy, second-class, Indian train. I was as comfortable as could be expected, lounging in my lofty bunk. I was enjoying my breezy new white pants and the pouch I wore around my neck as a substitute for pockets. For a view, I twisted around and could gaze out the open door from the end of my bunk, and marvel at how beautiful India was as its green fields, villages, and monsoon floods rolled by.

At each stop a parade of sellers, beggars, deformed people, and various hawkers would march or crawl by. I bought a vicious-looking knife from a guy for 5 rupees and gave a beggar lady a small coin. By about 6:00 p.m. we were in Varanasi.

People work hard to stir up some business from travelers and we rode on a rickshaw with one particular hard-working guy to check out his hotel. It didn't quite make it and we rickshawed back to the station. Varanasi is a bustling, thrown-together old town, the holiest and most full of pilgrims in India. The streets are clogged with thin, nearly naked people, bicycles, rickshaws, cows, and rarely a motor-driven vehicle, except for huge, old pre-war buses filled with pilgrims that look quite awkward in this situation. It looked like it would be hard to rise above this squalor without resorting to a very expensive hotel, but we would try to find something nice and clean but not extravagant.

First, we went to the central station and booked second-class sleeping berths to Agra ($4 each) and then we rickshawed around in search of the right hotel. We realized that Varanasi was not well endowed with tourist hotels and we decided the Hotel International was our best bet. We chose between two very spacious rooms: 45 rupees without air conditioning or 65 rupees with. We decided to be extravagant and take the air conditioning and now, as I write, I'm sitting in front of that wonderful machine. Cool.

Starved, we went downstairs and discovered their lousy dining room. It was so dark we couldn't see the food. Maybe that was best because, from the sound of the dirt crunching with each spoonful of rice in my mouth, I expect the food wasn't too good to look at. I'm getting tired of this dreary Indian food and the constant concern for hygiene. We both dream of a gluttonous homecoming. Back in our cool room, we supplemented our dinner with great peanut butter sandwiches and then went to bed early, so we could get up for our 5:30 tour in the morning.

Sunday, August 27: Varanasi

It was dark at 4:30 when we were "knocked up," as they say in England. What an ungodly hour! I took a quick shower, had some peanut butter and bread, put our padlock on the door, and went downstairs to meet two Parisians who were also going on the tour.

We rickshawed to the Tourist Bungalow and joined the tour that was forming. After a cup of tea and a bit of a wait, the tour picked up more tourists and we got underway. The reason it started so early was because sunrise is the hour of intense worship and rituals along the banks of the holy Ganga (Ganges) River. Every Hindu should make a pilgrimage at least once to this holy site. This is the best place to die, and thousands of old Hindus spend their last years here to do just that. Then it is fashionable to be cremated and have your ashes thrown into this sacred river.

We bused as close as we could and, after warnings about beggars, hawkers, and pickpockets, we filed out of the bus and marched single file, with a protective hand on our cameras and our heads high, trying not to see the misery and filth that carpeted the narrow alleyway we were following down to the sacred Ganges.

Hawkers tried desperately to sell their wares at ridiculously low prices, beggars looked as weak and miserable as possible, many showing rotten skin, scabs, or sores that were just swarming with bugs. Some people just sat motionless, head down, with a small pile of rice on their lap, hoping for more. Others held

Backpackers and pilgrims alike converge on the holy city of Varanasi on the holy river Ganges.

lifeless babies and some just ignored the world, pursuing good karma. We got to the milky shore of the Ganges and rustic old boats were waiting. We filled three boats with tourists and slowly worked our way upstream. Everyone on board had come to Varanasi for precisely this trip, and nearly everyone had cameras poised to take home images of this intense religious happening, that seems so strange to we Western Christians.

We came to the ghats, or stairs, which were mostly under the swollen waters of the Ganges. These people seemed at peace and thankful to be cleansing their bodies and souls in the filthy but supposedly healing water. Many had traveled across India for this bath. Many would never leave during this life. If they died here and had their ashes thrown into the river, they would escape the drudgery of reincarnation. They would rise above all that, reaching Nirvana, a kind of oneness with God, freeing oneself of individuality and egoism. People drink the water, jump into it, wash in it, do all kinds of rituals in it, or just sit in it. They all seemed very fulfilled, happy, and didn't care about the procession of wide-eyed, camera-toting tourists that filed by. I felt a bit rude treating their religious acts like an exhibit or a trip to the zoo, but I was very excited to witness this firsthand.

With poverty woven into everyday life, this trip gave me a new kind of souvenir: indelible images and important questions to struggle with.

Then we came to the dramatic climax of our morning tour: the place where bodies were cremated on open fires. We all knew it was here somewhere, but only after spotting the columns of black smoke did we know where. We actually got out of the boats and walked up to a viewpoint to see the bodies and fires. I snapped a pre-set picture and had to exit early with some angry Indians on my tail.

Walking back to the bus, we stopped by a golden temple and walked several powerful blocks through India at its grisliest, most shocking and, at the same time, richest. There's a lot of squalor and a lot of heartache in India. But there's also a lot of joy. I find I'm able to measure the land in terms of bulk joy (rather

Devout Hindus from across India make pilgrimages to the sacred waters of the Ganges. Travelers in small boats floated by the steps to observe faithful Hindus worshipping.

than joy per person) and perhaps that's why I see it as such a rich and wonderous—intoxicatingly wonderous—place.

Now, driving through the mob of jewelry-, flute-, incense-, and knife-sellers, we returned to the hotel area for breakfast. Gene and I decided to go first class and a had a great breakfast at Hotel de Paris for 12 rupees. We went back out at 8:50 a.m. with ten other tour members to meet the bus but found nothing but hungry rickshaw drivers very willing to act as the buses' substitutes. We figured the bus was just late but, one hour and a great dancing monkey show later, we all concluded we had been left and figured that was either rude or very stupid not to notice that twelve people from the bus had been left behind. We went to the tourist office en masse and the official there was very diplomatic and handled the whole thing, including one irate Frenchwoman who we had nicknamed "The Hammer," very tactfully and smoothly. A bus came after the tour finished and we got a personalized last half of the tour, with the only cost being the two-hour wait.

Our friendly guide enthusiastically showed us several temples. One was overrun with spoiled monkeys and I took the guide's warnings about them very seriously after my incident in Kathmandu. I hung on to my glasses, didn't look any of them in the eye, and stayed well away from the babies. Those monkeys were devilish. We also visited the huge and impressive Banaras Hindu University, where I saw the best and biggest temple I've seen in India. This one really impressed me architecturally.

The monsoon opened up in full fury, we fled into the bus, and happily made our way back to the hotels. After a rest and cooling-off with our air conditioner, we returned to the Tourist Bungalow Hotel and had a cheap and lousy lunch before our next tour left at 2:30 p.m.

An Italian girl caught my eye and kept my attention. I talked to her a bit but her English was as bad as my Italiano, so I settled for a pleasant afternoon of sightseeing. She really looked like Coconut (an Israeli draft dodger I once fell in love with on the road) but Gene perceptively saw Ruth (a long-time girlfriend I had recently broken up with) in her. Oh well, back to India.

We drove out of town to Sarnath, the place where Buddha gave his first sermon. For that reason, it's a very sacred place for Buddhists. Buddha preached here around 520 BC, and 300 years later the great Indian ruler Ashoka built a stupa, or monument, to Buddha. That can still be seen in Sarnath, as well as an archaeological museum that, for its one major piece, is worth the trip out there. That attraction is the symbol of India, the Lion Capital of Ashoka—a four-lioned pillar—and I was really enthralled by that old thing. It's on all the

money and stamps and now I stood before the real thing.

The rest of the museum was quite dull so I just followed the Italian girl around. Then we followed our guide to the ruins of an old monastery and a great Buddhist temple, where I carefully worked my way through a fresco that briefly told the story of Buddha.

Now it was teatime, and a banana, biscuits, and tea awaited our group in a nearby tourist lodge. We met an Australian girl named Sandra, who was in India studying music, and had a fun talk with her about intercultural meter and mode in the backseat of our bus as we drove to the other side of Varanasi to visit the Maharaja's Fort.

The fort provided us with our closest look at the lifestyle of the Maharajas during British rule. Museums showed us the elephant costumes, sedan chairs, bizarre weapons, and then we even got a look at a real-life Maharaja. The silly little band played horribly and a dilapidated circa-1955 car stood waiting as the word spread that the Maharaja was coming. All of us tourists readied our cameras and then he came. This was a living "dead" institution. His fort was a shambles, his band was embarrassing, and power and glory belonged only to his ancestors. I'm surprised his car started. After a quick look at the Ganges and a view of Varanasi across the river and downstream a ways, the tour was over and the bus took us home. We invited Sandra for a fancy dinner at the Hotel de Paris and agreed to pick her up around 8:00.

Our poor rickshaw driver had a broken bike, but he ran us home anyway and we relaxed, showered, I brushed my grimy teeth, and actually dressed up as best as I could. Then, feeling very clean and happy to widen our social circle to three, we took our motor-scooter to Sandra's place and then went to the doorstep of the Hotel de Paris. In India, an enjoyable environment is a very important part of the meal and here we had everything. I thought the Latin cha-cha music was out of place so they honored my request for Indian music and served us three wonderful meals for 55 rupees. That was a fun night, and we didn't get to sleep until too late but that was OK.

Monday, August 28: Varanasi

Oh, what good tourists we are! For the second morning in a row, we woke up at 4:30 a.m. and it was still dark as we motorscooter-rickshawed to the Ganges river. Without even asking for it, the hotel sent with us a young man

The maharaja still had his palace, his guard, and his limo— but it was all pretty comically run down.

eager to be our own personal guide and soldier of fortune.

Every tourist in this city is harried from dawn till dusk by people of all kinds who moonlight in the tourist business and see each tourist as a walking money tree. Harvest season lasts all year and the ultimate prize is the orchard: a tour group. Every rickshaw man, hotel worker, and riverboat boy seems to have a sitar teacher who knows Ravi Shankar and would love to play for us, a friend who will sell us silk for less than cost, a great little market for us to check out, and lots of other lies.

We asked to be taken to the Assi Ghat and this guy from our hotel just took us to the ghat (steps on the riverbank) where he would get a commission from the boatmen who would then take us to the Assi Ghat. The sun was warming the horizon and we wanted to be on the river for its first appearance. So, rather than fight it, we took a boat from there and rode up-river to the Assi Ghat and past many other busy ghats.

People were flocking to the river and, as the sun rose, bells rang and the religious activity intensified. It was nice to have our own boat, and our "guide" was actually helpful. We stopped at one special ghat and quietly observed the action. Gene put it well when he said that viewing like this was quite "philistine." Later we got a close and prolonged look at a cremation. With that, we were ready to get off this incredible river.

We escaped in a bit of commotion when I refused to give the boatman more than the 10 rupees we had agreed upon. Our "leader" then took us to hear sitar and tabla music. Shoes off and waiting for the inevitable sales pitch, we watched as two stylish-looking musicians warmed up and worked into a morning raga with a 16-beat tala. We didn't really know what was expected of us, so we just sat and enjoyed and learned, as they were happy to entertain questions between ragas. Later we were joined by a British family and heard some very good music.

Our scooter driver had been waiting for over two hours, and it was still before 8 a.m. We didn't want his or our "guide's" services anymore, so I rudely dismissed them and gave the rickshaw man 2 rupees for taking us where we didn't want to go and nothing for waiting. We walked away frustrated by their lousy business tactics and happy to be alone.

This was our chance to prowl around on our own and really saturate our senses with all the intensities of a Hindu's life along the Ganges. All kinds of flies and bugs adorned all kinds of crap that filled one kind of alley: dirty ones leading to the riverfront. We followed holy men down to the steps, where they waited as various pilgrims kissed their feet. We almost overdosed on the total experience: shriveled bodies clad in scanty rags, clinging to brass spittoon-like jars full of Ganges water; ladies dressed up in rich silk saris, drinking pensively in the swirling current; dark men wearing barely more than a penis-sheath, dropping flower petals; and women with pancake breasts, who were beyond caring about dumb things like covering your body. In an empty alley we would turn a corner and find ourselves face to face with a giant but meek cow. Fragrant breezes, tranced music, quivering flames, painted bodies, and cremations…it's all part of a visit to the milky Ganges.

We returned to our hotel where we were greeted once again by the staff, hopelessly and universally afflicted with dollar signs in their eyes. In the peace and coolness of our air-conditioned room, we sacked out. I was quite tired after less than five hours of sleep for the second night in a row. And I'll likely be just as tired tomorrow, after our long second-class overnight train ride tonight to Agra.

The back streets of Varanasi—the home of Lord Shiva and about two thousand temples—were intense.

At noon, we had some peanut butter sandwiches, and after a while, we stepped back out into the heat and caught a rickshaw to the bazaar area. It's really bad when your rickshaw driver doesn't know where he's going and pretends like he does. We finally just said stop. I gave him 2 rupees and he looked at me in a well-practiced look of astonishment and said "6." I told him he was crazy, put the 2 rupees on his knee, and walked off. The basic rule is if you don't draw complaints when you pay someone, you're overpaying them.

We were in a market area and spent a couple of hours walking and browsing. We found ourselves in a crazy human and bicycle traffic jam. The road was simply clogged to a standstill. Later we ventured into an industrial area, where dozens of boys and men pounded silver into paper-thin sheets for 12 hours a day, and there were also lock-makers, blacksmiths, and woodworkers. What we wanted to see, though, was the more touristy bazaar around the Golden Temple, where we could sample some of the local handicrafts.

We found this place just as the monsoon did and we jumped from the cover of one colorful and dripping shop to the next, splashing through a world of trinkets, blazing reds, elegant saris, and monsoon rain. I shopped around and bought two nice wall hangings, and then we hustled back to the Hotel International. After a quick shower, and smashing then de-meating my coconut with my Gurkha knife, I figured out how to fit everything into my stuffed rucksack, and we checked out of our hotel, caught a passing bike rickshaw, and said, "To the station, James."

The station restaurant was serving only omelets, bread, and tea so that was our dinner. By 6:30 we had found the seats labeled Openshaw and Steves and we were on our way to Agra. Second class ain't bad if it's a reserved car. Then you know there will be only one person per seat and no poor soul sprawled out under your seat. We had two pretty good window seats. The seats were hard and the windows were barred but we were rolling in the right direction and the stars were out.

I did some exercises in my lern-to-spell book and we played a little trip trivia before making up the bottom bunk (the top one was already ready), spreading a little padding in crucial spots on the hard wood, and then we tried to go to sleep.

Tuesday, August 29: Agra

The night was as long as the bed was hard. I couldn't stretch out and passed the night grabbing one-hour snatches of sleep. At 5 a.m. or so, I called it quits and made the seats back up just as we pulled into a little no-name station.

We waited in that station for over an hour and we figured we'd be very late for Agra but, right at 8:00, we pulled into the touristy city of the Taj Mahal. As usual, transportation and accommodations were absolutely no problem. Scores of overly helpful people were waiting like baby birds for their mothers' worms. Nobody was getting my worm and we marched through the mob and down the street, to get beyond the hustlers and hopped on a rickshaw not waiting to gouge a backpacker for a ride to the tourist office. It was closed so we had the guy carry on to the nearby Grand Hotel which, from our information, looked to be about what we wanted for what we had to spend.

We took a nice, big, clean, air-conditioned room, with a complete bathroom and breakfast, for 75 rupees (about $9.50) and went down for breakfast. This was great: We were all set up and it was only 8:30 a.m. A nice hotel and a very nice, relatively clean, and wealthy city would be ours for two days.

There was a 10:30 all-day tour today and we decided we might as well get busy and take it. And for 17 rupees each, we boarded the "ordinary bus." The "deluxe bus" was air-conditioned, included cold drinks, cost twice as much, and was filled with Westerners. Most of the people on our tour were Indians who had come down from Delhi on the Taj Express and were making Agra a day trip.

First, we drove 30 kilometers out of town to a deserted palace city called Fatehpur Sikri that Emperor Akbar had built. It took years and millions of man hours to build, and Akbar abandoned it after a few years for lack of water. That left an eerie, impressive ghost town that, 400 years later, tourists would wander through, being chased by hawkers and beggars. It was huge and beautiful! Nice Mughal architecture by any standards. We saw the harem, the parcheesi board that used sexy maidens for pieces, and a huge complex of royal buildings, all out in the middle of Indian nowhere. After touring the big mosque, we loaded back into our "ordinary bus" and returned to Agra for lunch. I was really feeling my sleep deficit and slept most of the dusty way back.

After lunch and checking out some lousy emporiums (government souvenir shops), we returned to the bus. I passed time, as one does when waiting for a bus to go, by bargaining with the many aggressive merchants out my window. Show interest (just a glance at their junk does it) and then you'll weather the barrage of rattles, wooden snakes, faded postcards, bananas, peacock fans, and jewelry that tries to find its way through the window. As the bus begins to roll, the merchants actually run with it, still trying to close a deal through the window.

We rolled on to the big Agra Fort. This red fort, built in 1565 by Akbar, the grandfather of Shah Jahan who built the Taj Mahal, is better, I think, than Delhi's Red Fort. We toured it, getting a great view of the Taj just down the Yamuna River, and seeing many of the lavish buildings housed inside the two-mile long and 70-foot-high wall. Gardens, well-watered plants, the river, and a cool fresh breeze made the fort a pleasant place for an afternoon visit.

Then a guy asked Gene if they had met before. He was Shaun Sullivan from Seattle. He went to Seattle Prep, then Stanford, and was now at the UW Medical School. He had met Gene five years ago, washing dishes in a Stanford dorm. Great coincidence and a happy one. Shaun is a very nice guy, and we had a fun afternoon together and, for once, we had a travel friend who we wouldn't be saying goodbye forever to in a few hours. We'll get together in Seattle this fall.

The last part of our tour and, a highlight for sure, was the famous Taj Mahal. This marble tomb was built from 1631 to 1653 by 20,000 laborers for one lady, Mumtaz Mahal. She was the wife and love of Shah Jahan, the fourth Mughal ruler since Babur, and apparently quite a guy.

Our guide gave us the rundown on the place, and we were free to roam and soak in its beauty any way we wanted. I was blown away by the gentle harmony of the beautiful marble dome, minarets, gardens, and ponds. This was probably number one on my list of things to see and now it's right up there with the Kremlin and Versailles on my list of favorite sights of all time. It was simply beautiful, more beautiful than any postcard or picture could ever be. You must stand there and let your eyes play up and down its graceful yet strong lines. The Taj is not something to be rushed. We let the tour go on without us and lingered, watching the setting sun shape the lines and shadows and warm up the white of the marble surfaces. We walked around the lush gardens, catching it from different angles. The inside wasn't really special. A couple of modest tombs under a tomb, but from the outside the Taj Mahal is everything.

I thought for years that it would probably be smaller than I imagined, dusty, cramped by neighboring buildings, surrounded by an unkempt, burned-off garden, cluttered with beggars, hawkers, animals, and swarming with tourists, sweating under a merciless sun. It was absolutely none of that. I can always go back to the Taj and be thrilled.

We stepped out for a cold drink and returned to sit on the grass, with chipmunks and red horizons, and just soaked it in. The lovely Taj Mahal.

We decided to have dinner with Shaun and, after a great shower and that rare clean feeling, he came over to our hotel and we went down for dinner. We had a great evening. Shaun told us good stories about his experiences in Sri Lanka and we reciprocated with bits and pieces from "The Hippie Trail to Kathmandu." We got the waiter to stifle the cheap disco music and put on something

Indian. I finally tried the popular drink called sweet lassi, a yogurt drink, and I'll have to have more. We traded addresses, agreed to get together in Seattle, and said goodbye as he stepped into his waiting rickshaw. We went up to Room 33 and went straight to bed. We have to get up at 5 a.m. for the fourth morning in a row, and our sleep deficit is taking me from Sleepy to Dopey.

Wednesday, August 30: Agra

At 5 a.m. I was far, far away, the banging door caused Gene to slug me, and I yelled "Okay, good morning!" trying to sound awake enough to convince the guy he could stop knocking. Then we slept on. At 6 a.m. the door started making that same noise again. This time it was the taxi driver we had ordered last night. He had been waiting for 30 minutes. We realized what we had done, jumped into our clothes, and in five minutes we were heading back to the Taj Mahal.

We wanted to catch the sunrise but this morning was very cloudy and the only thing anyone was catching was the sprinkling rain. We were disappointed but still wanted to see the Taj while the tourists were still sleeping. We walked through the gate to that great white monument of love…it was silent, pristine, and all ours.

Eventually a few fanatic photographers and the sweeper broke the sleepy calm. The clouds were dark with a light stripe on the horizon and raindrops obliterated the reflections in the pond, but it was still nice to sit and ponder my favorite tomb at this hour.

After a while, we took a three-wheeler back to the Grand Hotel and had breakfast. ABBA played on the stereo, and I got the waiter to augment my ridiculous bowl of cereal (called Corn Flex here) with some fresh fruit.

After breakfast, we returned to the room and I realized that we were both getting a bit weird and jaded at this late date in the trip. Every day we find ourselves saying, "Only so many more days till we board that plane in Frankfurt."

We were tired after getting up so early and we had to check out by noon. Neither of us had much intention of doing anything until then. Determined to catch up in the journals and write our last "I'm coming home!" postcards, we snoozed and wrote for a while. I had a good, long shower and then we invented a baseball game where a fan actually got a chance to bat. Lying on the bed, we crumpled up pieces of an Indian map and lobbed them over into the swinging blades of the fan. If it fell through cleanly, it was a strike, and then different hits were called singles, doubles, and so on depending on where the fan whacked the balled-up paper "ball." After three innings, Tissue led the Wrinkles, 3 to 2.

By noon, we packed up and checked out. I bought a good-looking little Indian history book and Gene picked up a book on Hindu mythology. We stopped in our cute little restaurant for a lunch of omelet, rice, sweet lassi, and 17 "finger chips" (French fries). By now it was getting into the afternoon and we had to get moving. We settled our bill: $18 for the room, four meals each, and some little extras.

Then we took the famous Alauddin rickshaw man downtown. We had to read his book of flattery and foreign addresses (like Muzaffar's of Kashmir) and I managed to write some hogwash praising the dumb guy. It's a pity that nice guys get the least pay and turkeys like Alauddin manage to kick and stomp more money out of the tourists.

We freed ourselves in the Kinari Bazaar and spent a couple of aimless hours absorbing the rich atmosphere. I got a nice Indian leather watch band from a genuinely nice guy, who made me feel good. We floated in and out of various neighborhoods. Shoe stores with prices that looked like dollars but were only rupees, such as 8.95, 13.95, and so on.

Small primitive industries were busy being industrious: hay pounders, paper printers, box makers, steel-pole pounders, and melon squeezers making a gross-looking juice. We walked through a sickeningly sweet-smelling bazaar, passing a guy so thin he looked like a concentration camp victim. Then I noticed a swastika painted on the wall behind him. That has been a Hindu symbol for centuries, before Hitler was even born, long before people associated it with Nazis. Swastika is actually a Sanskrit word.

Next, we came to some big stinking pigs. These pigs were so gross we both concluded that they totally deserve their bad reputation. Wallowing in a mountain of rotten melons, treating the bugs like sugar, and just rutting away happily.

Later, we found ourselves on literally the bad side of the train tracks amid horses, cows, broken rickshaws, and so much junk, pressure from hustlers, and noise. Needing a quick change of scene, we just hopped on a rickshaw after a while and retreated to the peaceful lawn chairs of our hotel garden.

Just when we were ready for dinner, the wicked monsoon chased us into the dining room. We took our time eating and by 6:00 p.m. we realized we could be missing our 6:45 train. The fastest rickshaw around was summoned. Gene and I were in fantastic spirits as our hair danced down the smiling streets of Agra. We sang our heads off, waved and joked with passing Indians, and enjoyed our driver's company. We gave him a whopping 5 rupees and it felt good to make him feel good.

The station was a scene of "refugee camp" chaos. In the commotion, all kinds of colorful people flickered in the station lights—which created puddles of shining silk and cotton. Strangely the light caused nose rings, ankle bracelets, and teeth inlaid with precious metals to sparkle. Dark eyes followed us as we wondered what track our train was on.

Somewhere along Track 3 we found Mr. Steves and Mr. Openshaw listed on the reservation notices on a car. Exploring our car, we found wooden padding on the 4'10" "long" beds. They looked more like empty cupboards than beds. Oh well, this is India and I really accepted this funny situation gracefully as I climbed awkwardly into my top bunk, with six or eight pairs of dark eyes following my every move.

I finally positioned myself, feet resting on the next bed, folded jeans padding my tailbone, and head on my poncho, and lost myself in the modern Indian history book I had bought today.

At about 11:00 p.m. my lids got heavy and I put the book away. Time flipped by in one-hour snatches, as I laid on one side until sore and then switched to the other. By 3:00 we were in Jaipur. Our only desire was to salvage some sleep tonight and we let a little rickshaw boy take us to the Teej Tourist Bungalow, where we crashed in the dormitory for 5 rupees each.

Thursday, August 31: Jaipur, the Pink City

In a dorm situation, everyone wakes up at the same time, and this morning that time was 7 a.m. I felt pretty good, considering the wacky night's sleep I got, and Gene and I wasted no time in beginning our last search for a hotel.

Hotel finding is about the hardest work I have to do when I'm traveling, except possibly for writing in this book, and we kind of celebrated the fact that, after tonight, every night left is already arranged. This last search was to be one of our most difficult. We wanted a moderate splurge—one last splurge—but everything in our range was either not good enough or full. We tried every place on the tourist office's list and even, accidentally, a "home for sick people" that wasn't on the list. I fell in love with that place from a distance, but I got over that in a hurry when I saw the clientele.

Finally, we came to the Khetri House, where the Maharaja of Khetri stays when he's in Jaipur. It was a stately, if a bit decrepit, old mansion and, at first, we weren't too impressed. Then the quiet court yard, big garden, huge room completely furnished, waiting room, big bathroom, abundance of servants, and the peace—the extreme lack of busy-ness, with only tropical birds chirping—grew on us. I said yes to the 77 rupees ($9.50) price for a double suite with two big breakfasts, while Gene still wavered. He's always glad after I push a splurge; we are really enjoying this fantastic life.

When you rent a Maharaja's palace, it comes with wheels at your beck and call.

We explored the three-room suite and realized we were the total kings of this maharaja's palace. There was no one else here—only me, Gene, and a dozen hired hands to cook our eggs, call the rickshaw, trim the gardens, and offer to do our laundry. We relaxed and then sat down in the lavish, huge, and empty dining room for a big, typical, breakfast.

Happily settled, we called for a rickshaw, crossed Chandpole Gate, and entered the old, pink city of Jaipur. Then, as if to welcome us, the sky opened up, and the next three hours were washed away in a long, long monsoon downpour.

There we sat, drenched, under a skimpy tarp in the only rickshaw in Jaipur without a canopy. Crazy Baba, with a scrapbook of friends and pictures from all over the world, and mud caked on his long black hair, jived as he pedaled us through the rain. We hustled with him straight for the museum and, totally drenched, took refuge in rooms of old Mughal paintings, sedan chairs, artifacts, and military equipment. We explored the city palace and exhausted the museum, and the rain still came down. We taxied to the Grand Emporium and shopped for a while. I bought a tiny little garnet (semi-precious stone) for 6p and the poor shopkeeper had to go through ridiculous red tape to sell the thing. Nothing else really appealed to us there and the rain continued, so we took a short ride over to another museum and spent some time learning about the desert state of Rajasthan and drying out.

I could feel something different in this town. The main center of Rajasthan, Jaipur is full of beautiful streets, buildings, and people. The people are really special. Very colorful, happy, quick with a warm smile, and the women are the most beautiful women I've seen in India. The people of Rajasthan also have a fun sense of humor. This place makes me want to explore more of India and its people.

After lunch in a very modern, busy, pleasant, and totally vegetarian restaurant, we spent the rest of the day just enjoying the fascinating pink streets of Jaipur. What a place! Camel trains ambling slowly and carelessly down the main street; a dark, hairy fat man standing stark naked in his doorway, while six monkeys ignore him and perch on the roof; bikes, cows, and rickshaws clogging the streets; ladies sitting in a sea of flowers, selling garlands. Beggars with missing or curly dwarfed limbs clambered down muddy roads, pushing tin cups of coins with their mud-caked heads, while green parrots perched on

Beggars, intentionally deformed by their parents at birth, go to work daily like this.

their sides cackled. Kids surrounded the pathetic pairs of scooting beggars, pleading with us to take pictures of the bizarre scene.

A rickshaw driver assured us that a crumpled camel lying in the road was just sleeping. He didn't breathe. Merchants sold bananas, coconuts, leaf-rolled cigarettes rubber-banded in groups of ten, and sugar cane juice.

I stopped in a shop that I thought might have the after-dinner herb anise, and the guy whipped out the hashish and ganja of Shiva that was sold openly right on the street. We picked up five grams for 3 rupees (35 cents). After a tough decision, I picked out two wooden-block-dyed bed sheets that I will try to make into a comforter cover at home. I also bought a pair of ankle bracelets to give someone at home. Now's that time of the trip when I have to make sure I have something for everyone at home. I don't quite know why, but I like to bring something home on every trip for each person in my family.

It had stopped raining and the temperature was actually comfortable. We were in tremendous spirits as we headed back to our hotel, wishing today wasn't over so fast, but marveling at how long ago yesterday seemed. We bought flower leis on the way home and just lived it up, joking with the people we passed, singing, and I knew that Jaipur was a place to come back to.

With only four more days left in India, that sense of urgency, that "time is running out and soon it will be gone; enjoy it while you have it" feeling has overcome me, and I really want these last days to be good ones.

At 7:00 p.m. we entered the gates and walked down the lane that led through the forested estate to the Khetri House. How jolly good this was. The servants and singing birds greeted us and we found our room bigger and better than ever. We sent Lord Shiva some ganja smoke signals and took a very interesting walk in the dark garden. Suddenly, the shadows and distant voices were wonderful in the cool, star-filled breeze. We sat on the royal porch of the Maharaja's and looked out. Then a funny "accredited" fortune teller entertained us but failed to draw any money out of us. After a few more minutes, we were told that "dinner was prepared."

In the dining room, two places out of 30 were set. We sat down and the servants brought on the food. The dinner of mutton, potatoes, pumpkin soup (aka "Indian soup"), and banana pudding was fine and the company was funny. When they were done serving us, all the boys from the kitchen gathered around to watch us eat. I suggested that a fifth guy, who was standing in the background, pull up a chair and join the party.

Over coffee and pudding, we got into an interesting conversation with the hotel staff covering family planning, castration, Indira Gandhi, political parties, and wives. They don't like Communists, families of more than five kids, castration, or China. They wondered why we hadn't married yet and they insisted we were rich. After a while, we said goodnight to the servants we share with the Maharaja of Khetri and went up to our suite and to bed.

Friday, September 1: Jaipur to Delhi

Breakfast was served to the pummeling rhythm of the pouring monsoon. Today was a big day and we hoped for dry weather. The hot milk made my Corn Flex instantly mush but breakfast was fine. After a few documentary shots capturing our fleeting splendor, we left our friends at the Maharaja's place and took a rickshaw through the great pink stone gate and to the center of the old town, where a bus was waiting to take us to the Amber Fort, 11 kilometers down the road toward Delhi.

After a while, huge, lumbering elephants appeared on the road and we came to a small town below a great, fortified hilltop. This was Amber and it greeted us with a terrible downpour. Like everyone else, we took shelter with cows and monkeys under an over-hanging eve. In a stunning admission of where they ranked on the animal hierarchy of "who cares about filth," only the gross pigs went about their muddy business, oblivious to the rain. There we stood, enjoying a world painted and shaped by monsoon streaks and drizzles. Tall, thin tarps splashed by, children were dwarfed by big black umbrellas, the street became a river, and passing cars sprayed a brown wake. I stared at a monkey and he went scampering across the roof and peeked in from the other side. Hanging with the cows, we waited for the rain to let up.

When we got the chance, we went up to the elephant yard and saw the tourists loading on in fours, to be carried heavily up the hill to the fort. Standing in the shelter of a souvenir shop, we decided that we were here more to ride an elephant than see another fort and, in this weather, the cheaper jaunt through the marketplace would suffice. This way we paid only 5 rupees instead of 12 rupees each and had only two people on the beast's back plus the driver, who sat on the elephant's head with a mean-looking spike to steer with. The rain slowed down and Gene and I climbed the little concrete loading tower to "board" our elephant. This was exciting, something that for years has been very high on my checklist of things to do. I read about this three years ago and underlined it in triple in my guidebook, knowing that someday I would come to Jaipur and check this out. We swayed and rocked high above the streets of Amber, holding the umbrellas above us and soaking in this experience with help of the persistent rain. What fun! We took turns riding solo and taking pictures of each other. Once, as the elephant was coming in for a "landing," I was riding side-saddle and just got my legs out of the way before the elephant's hide crushed against the concrete. That could easily have turned this dream into a nightmare, as my frail little legs would have stood about the same chance as a worm under my boot.

That was 10 rupees well spent and now we stood in the drizzle and tried to flag down a ride to Delhi. I felt awkward hitching Indian-style, which isn't sticking out your thumb but waving your hand in a downward motion, but you do what you have to do. After about 30 minutes, a big truck stopped and the Sikh at the wheel said to get in; he was going to Delhi. I thought it would be too crowded but we managed to fit five men and our two rucksacks into the front seat and we were on our way. (The cab was so big, I sat between the driver and his door.) In India, so much is "makeshift," broken but working smoothly through what my Dad taught me was "field expediency" and this truck was no exception. The starter was a loose wire, the window on one side was a plastic pillow, a bolt kept the glove compartment shut, and colorful pictures of Hindu gods decorated the cab, keeping us out of the ditch.

Goin' my way?

We plugged along at a rate of about 30 miles per hour and we were 150 miles out of Delhi. That was a good day's ride. The rain came down as we rolled steadily past floods, hordes of vultures, grazing and hauling camels, women decorating brown wells with rainbows of laundry, and overturned trucks. There were lots of accidents, but we seemed to be going very safely. We stopped for a break about a third of the way to Delhi: They gave us tea and we shared our glucose biscuits. Then a bus stopped just down the road. When we found out that the bus was Delhi-bound, we decided (just for a new experience and a change of scene) to say thank you and namaste to our truck friends and pile into the bus.

The bus just sat there in the big puddles for a while and the Sikh truck driver's parting words of "We will arrive in Delhi first" rang in my ears. But when every seat on the bus was full, we paid our 10 rupees each and took off. This bus flew—no stops, no animals, not even anyone standing in the aisle. The 160 kilometers ticked away as we splashed through rivers rushing over the road.

With the rain still pouring down, and my watch reading 5:00 p.m., we entered the capital city. Delhi was having its wettest day of the year and the temperature was nine degrees below normal at 77 degrees. We felt good to be coming into a city we knew; it's so much easier than a new place. We knew just what to do.

Just as we got off the bus, an incredible sea of rain poured wildly down. There was no shelter except a waiting bus, so we took refuge in that. After a while, we boarded a three-wheel scooter and cruised over to the flooded Imperial Hotel. The friendly student travel office was still open and happy to help

With the monsoon came flooding. Hitching a ride on a big truck, fording raging rivers seemed routine to our driver.

us. We wanted to confirm our flight and they said no problem and brought us tea. We also found that the rains had cancelled the Haridwar-Rishikesh tour (where we had hoped to go for our last days in India) so we had three days to relax in Delhi.

We were wet, tired, and hungry. It was great to have our familiar YMCA to check into. We took a rickshaw "home" through the rain and checked into a double down the hall from, but exactly the same, as our old room. Just like the last time we arrived in Delhi, the first thing we did was lay out all of our rain-drenched stuff. I picked up the bag we had left here and laid all my souvenirs out to play with. I had collected a fascinating array of stuff—it's like a Rudyard Kipling Christmas!

After a rest we went down for dinner, ordering and sharing one Western and one Indian meal. I'm so glad I learned to make dessert out of my rice by adding milk and sugar. (I always order coffee so I get milk and sugar for my rice.)

Rained in, we kind of goofed the rest of the night away in our room, playing baseball with the fan, reading, writing, and relaxing. I didn't get tired until quite late, long after Gene had fallen asleep.

Saturday, September 2: Delhi

Yesterday was the wettest day of India's year and today was only a little better. After a good breakfast with great porridge, I took a long, hot shower and we were ready to brave the rain. We planned rainy-day sights, but first we wanted to confirm our London flight. Thai Airways had our names on the flight list and everything was in good order. That really eased my mind. (I was obsessed with the thought that, had we been scammed by the "bucket shop" that sold us our tickets, we'd have no money to leave India. That would have been another journal entirely.) Now I know that Tuesday morning at 8:30 we will be in London—Europe, halfway to Seattle!

Our first sight for today was the National Gallery of Modern Art and, with no reason to hurry, we took our time and really enjoyed this look at contemporary Indian culture. Gene and I studied each room, picture by picture, and came up with our favorites. Only rarely did our choices match but we both agreed that was a good museum. I like seeing a museum by playing this game. You get more out of the paintings by sharing evaluations.

Next, with the rain persisting, we took in the National Museum. This big place was quite dull. I have such a hard time getting into such a foreign archaeology and such ancient art forms. The sculptures and paintings seemed so crude next to contemporaneous Classical Greek or Roman works. I hope I'm not guilty of ethnocentrism. We finished this museum in a rather abbreviated form and decided not to wait for the free 2:30 p.m. film, which would probably just be the museum again but on the screen—even duller!

Outside we had an impossible time, for some reason, securing a free or empty rickshaw. Finally, we gave up and walked to a bus stop and hopped on, not knowing where it was going but at least it was going somewhere. As I suspected, it went to the hub, Connaught Circus, and from there, after a light lunch in a very fancy "shirt and tie" type restaurant, we caught a rickshaw to the old bazaar: Chandni Chowk. Except for on our city tour, this was the first time we'd been in Old Delhi. I was getting tired of the relatively big-city-modernness of New Delhi, so Old Delhi was really refreshing. We wide-eyed our way through crowded streets, working our way deep into the dark and fragrant innards of the bazaar area.

Bazaars are great and Old Delhi's was no exception. We watched cigarettes being rolled by hand—tobacco wrapped in a leaf that sold for 3 cents a pack; sat in to look at some fancy embroidery; enjoyed a photogenic sign that read simply, "Sex Disorders"; ducked through jungles of silk saris and glittering sashes; dodged hurried bicycle rickshaws; and peered down dark alleys. We also checked out an Indian music store. I got

a chance to play a dreary pump-organ-like harmonium, and we were both turned on by a sitar. I didn't realize that good sitars could be had for under $100 and I suddenly, along with Gene, found myself in the market for a sitar. We checked several stores, finding sitars for $25 and up. Back on Connaught Circus, I heard one and tried it out (terribly) that was truly exceptional. It cost $100. This would be something to think about.

By now it was after 6:00 p.m. and we had time only for a quick stop at the Y before taxiing over to the Asoka Hotel to hear Jagjit Singh and his wife, Chitra Singh, perform a recital of ghazal music. These are musical love poems and the artists, apparently, are among India's finest. Again, we had trouble finding an available rickshaw and we had to resort to a more expensive taxi. The Asoka Hotel was rich and huge, very first-class, and the concert hall sat 3,000 under chandeliers and over red carpets. The show, scheduled for 7:00 p.m., didn't start until 8, but we occupied ourselves with a study of the Indian high society class that filled this hall. Many beautiful girls, wealthy men, and proud Sikhs—with their turbans and chin-strap beards—were all around. While there were also a few tourists and a few resident Westerners, this was basically an Indian event for Indians.

The primary reason for coming to this recital was to enjoy the lyrics. The music was good, but the lyrics were exceptional. At 8:00, the two stars and their four or five accompanying musicians sat cross-legged on the stage and began a tight, tender, and very "laid-back" performance. Each player was very aware of the others and subtlety was the key. Sadly, there was no sitar or veena, but we heard the same old harmonium, tabla, and flute combination.

We left early to get dinner and because 45 minutes of ghazal music is ample for any mortal Western tourist. After dinner, we got into a pretty heavy discussion about cultural virtues and what is "cultured," comparing the mountain shepherds we visited in Kashmir to American poets and intellectuals. After a little fan baseball, we hit the sack.

Sunday, September 3: Delhi

Well, for once, we woke up to sunny skies. I guess Sundays are pretty similar worldwide because this was the "closed and quiet" day in Delhi. For a tourist running out of time, this is not desirable.

With breakfast, we enjoyed the strange and funny English-language Delhi newspaper, laughing at the esoteric crossword puzzle clues (e.g. "Direction for a parachutist with a dicky heart, about to play a snooker shot") and the matrimony section of the classifieds ("Homely daughter of millionaire, 165 cm, caste no bar") and minor headlines ("Tribesmen flog a vehicle, we hear").

Our goal for today was to check out an Indian village…a village that had never seen a Westerner in person. My theory was that Sunday loses its significance in the countryside. I relish the challenge of getting somewhere the hard way—just taking anything rolling in the general direction and working my way confidently along the road until I reach my destination. Gene usually warily cautions me, "I don't know if anything will stop." We could have gone to a central terminal and caught a direct bus, but instead we rickshawed to the Delhi-Agra highway and hitched and bused along the road. After a pleasant and airy ride in the back of a truck, we were let off at the Jaitpur village cut-off. We headed down the dusty road, looking for Molarband, a charming (as in snake-charming) little hamlet behind the village of Jaitpur.

A Shave and a Crowd

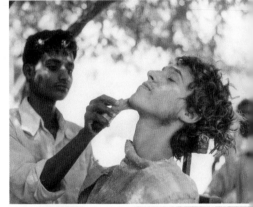

Gene had been growing a beard with little success for eight weeks and now was the time for the meager harvest. He wanted to shave it off Indian-style and now we stumbled into the perfect barber shop. Under a tree on the roadside, a guy was just finishing up with a customer and he welcomed Gene into his chair. I sat down on a cot, ready to enjoy this event and, very quickly, a crowd gathered.

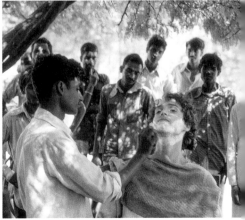

Gene was lathered up and, with a razor-sharp blade, the villager (probably a barber by caste) moved Gene's beard and moustache from his face to a foamy pile on the side of the barber's left hand. The crowd really enjoyed the show. I think the barber got the biggest thrill of all and, after leaving him 2 rupees, Gene walked away with a very good shave—and looking much better too.

Tourists visit a little village...

Everyone in Delhi tried to talk us out of visiting a village. They said it was bad during the monsoon and not very interesting. We both really wanted a close look at a typical village before leaving this country and we were quickly running out of time. (I had actually designed my own for-credit course a year ago at the University of Washington called "Village India.") I felt like I had been doing too much city-hopping and India is basically a village society, with only 10 or 15% of its massive population residing in big cities. Here in a village, we hoped to catch a glimpse of a more traditional, pure aspect of Indian culture.

From Molarband, we rode the raggy bus to the end of the line for 1.5 cents and got off in the middle of mud-brick huts, outdoor cot beds, wells, muddy white and lazy cows, and plenty of curious people. This was Jaitpur. A village that probably doesn't know what tourism is. Not a hotel, not a restaurant, not a painted house, not a car, not a paved road, and not an English-speaking person anywhere.

The thing to do in a village is to walk slowly through it, waving at the people who have looked out their doors to see you, and peering into courtyards. We walked across Jaitpur until we came to the green fields, and then worked our way around the fringe of the village. Mostly I felt very foreign, snapping pictures with kind of a guilty feeling until we were invited into a hut. This is just what you hope for when exploring a village, and now we had a chance to get a firsthand look at a village home. Half the village, eagerly staring at us, followed us in. We accepted but didn't want the chai (tea) they offered.

That's always a problem: to be a gracious guest without getting sick on the food and drink you're offered. Tea always looks as dangerous as its setting, but we sipped away. We passed a pack of glucose biscuits around and, reluctant to accept their food, I saw the children excitedly tear into them outside. All this time I was trying my best to communicate with the uniformed and dignified man who apparently was our host. We had absolutely no words in common, but we still smiled and babbled away without communication.

I was happy to get a good look at a village living situation. I think every visitor to India should check out a real village. After a while, we felt that maybe we were wearing our welcome thin. Besides, sitting on that bed with everyone staring at us was getting kind of old. We excused ourselves and walked around the village some more until we were saturated and ready to return to the 20th century.

On the road out of town we came upon four beautiful women carrying huge baskets of grass on their heads. I goofed around with them a bit, discovering that they had a sense of humor, and then I made my move. Crouching under the giant hat of hay, I looked the bubbly lady right in the eye as I straightened up, relieving her of her burden. The load was heavy, but I had so much fun as part of the group transporting what must be cow food down the road.

I gave the lady back her grass and we walked on, catching a ride later in a Jeep. On the main road we crushed into one of the local buses. The guidebooks recommend to never venture into these sardine tins on wheels but I think it's a tremendous experience. Muscling our way in and then asking where the bus was heading, I found myself in a crazy tangle of humanity. It was, in a strange way, fun. You abandon any sense of "personal space," and everyone just hangs and sits and climbs on everyone else. I stayed in the back and watched the daredevils cling to the doorway at each stop, hoping things would loosen up so they could work their way inside as the heavy-laden bus sped down the road.

I felt like I was playing Twister as I weaseled and wormed my way to the front of the bus. At just the right moment, as the bus slowed down, Gene and I jumped off and everything was suddenly peaceful. After savoring the remote and totally real corner of India we had reached, we caught a rickshaw and, in very high spirits, returned home for a much-needed rest and lunch.

We eat at least two meals a day at our YMCA. We have a feud boiling briskly between us and the waiters and it gets worse with each meal. Neither we nor they are doing anything to ease the situation. I think there's a certain element of pride and stubbornness involved. The root of the problem is probably our strange habits. We like more than two slices of toast in the morning. We need our coffee or tea with, not after, the meal. We need water, preferably in a pitcher, so we can put our iodine in it. We split everything so we can taste twice as many dishes. I eat my rice out of their sacred serving bowl with milk and sugar. We keep demanding service, and they keep trying not to give it. If I get up to get the water jug or find

Hey! I mean, hay! Can I lighten your load?

some sugar, they really get shook up. The food is clean, cheap, and edible—meeting all of our requirements—so we continue to eat and fight at the Delhi YMCA.

After the meal we went up to rest and play an inning or two of fan baseball. Our room is so full of crumpled up paper baseballs, that we carry the key with us every day so the floor boy can't come in to clean. I lay down and when I opened my eyes, it was three hours and some great dreams later. I didn't really mind the lost time. Both Gene and I are happy with what we've seen in India and now we are more or less relaxing and waiting for our flight to London.

We did go out to find a movie that wasn't sold out and made reservations for tonight at 9:30. Then it was back to the Y for dinner. On the way home we stopped by the Free Church of Delhi for the evening service.

I had read about a 6:30 p.m. English church service on the YMCA bulletin board and thought that sounded like a good idea. I hadn't been to an English church service all summer and Delhi seemed like a good place to enjoy one. We walked in during a hymn and found a very small, mostly Indian, congregation singing while the organist fumbled along very slowly under a whirling fan. Then the woman pastor in a snow-white veil outfit read the lessons and so on with a strict Puritan manner and a terse English accent. She looked straight to the side so we saw only her profile. She didn't do much for me, but her strength and dedication were impressive. It must be hard to run a Christian church in a land so full of Hindu and Buddhist traditions. I met some very nice people, and after the service, I had tea with a man from Bombay. He was an herbal medicine middleman and told us about rose petals boiled in sweet milk (for tourist stomach, aka Delhi Belly) and I also got a short lecture on the seriousness of

Cinema is huge in India and provides the traveler with a handy break from the intensity of the streets.

venereal disease. VD is the last of my worries when I'm traveling in India, unless you can pick it up from the rickshaw seats.

Back at the Y, it was dinnertime and we enjoyed a chance to try an Indian specialty, tandoori chicken. It was nothing special, but we had fun fighting with the waiters. Our plan for the evening was to see our third Hindi movie. The movie we saw was entertaining, even though we couldn't understand a word all night. The love scenes were corny, the fight scenes made the 1960s Batman TV show look realistic, and the musical aspect of the film was really catchy, even beautiful. I've become attached to Indian film music. Film is the medium for Indian pop music. The people can hear their favorite singers and watch their favorite actors and actresses lip sync the songs while enjoying the crazy predictable romantic plots. The people really get into these films and, for 2 or 3 rupees, they get more than their money's worth. So did we. Sneakily eating our popcorn (it's not allowed inside), we stayed until the finish and capped our day with a slow bicycle-rickshaw ride through the quiet city and back to the YMCA.

Monday, September 4: Delhi

Today was our last day in India and just that fact made it an exciting day. When I got up, I had the day's business on my mind. We had to pack, check out, reconfirm our flight to London, visit a huge mosque, and spend the rest of our Indian money. We did everything—and more.

After breakfast we checked our luggage, having stuffed all my souvenirs into our cute little green suitcase we picked up for our purchases. Then we went out to find a sitar. After touring a mean mosque that I didn't like, we found a rather large music store and tried out their sitars. When I came in, I was of a mind to spend about $100 for a very nice sitar but I played some $50 ones that sounded fine and I decided that, at least until I learn a little more about the sitar, one of these more modest models would be fine.

Gene and I played three, all priced at 350 rupees, and all a little different. After much listening and comparing, I found the one I liked and started talking prices. I wanted the works: extra strings, picks, extra bowl, a hard case, and instruction books for 400 rupees, or about $50. He was reluctant but I knew he'd find his way down to close the deal. I ended up getting everything but the two books for $50 and paid $5 for the books. I followed my Indian baby into the shop and watched with fatherly concern while the craftsman attached the second bowl for me. I walked down the stairs and into the busy street, excited about my new toy and the whole world of new music that I now had the key to. The question remains: Will I work at it or will I lose interest and just end up storing the sitar? I can hardly wait to show my Dad (who imports pianos from Europe), he'll get a kick out of it.

Now we had lunch back at the Y and spent the afternoon shopping. Gene doesn't buy souvenirs so I felt like maybe I was dragging him along, but I was having a blast. I had cashed $10 more than we needed and now I was obligated to spend it. Ten dollars goes a long way in India so I had my work cut out for me. I managed to blow the works and by 7:00 p.m., when we returned to the Y, I had a white Indian shirt and pants, a pair of harem pants for my girlfriend Vickie, and a dress for Mom, two tiger pens, three cheap little padlocks, a pair of sunglasses, and a family of five tiny carved rosewood elephants.

I was a sweaty pit when I sat down for my last Indian supper. I felt like I had jungle rot or something in my left armpit and I could hardly wait for a shower. But first we had one last bone to pick, so to speak, with the waiters. This was to be the finale, the showdown. Both sides were ready. We took our seats and couldn't get water. Our coffee didn't come until after the meal. And when I poured milk and sugar on my rice and spooned into the serving bowl, not only our waiter but two of his cohorts as well sprung to our table and asked the head waiter to do something about us. He tried to smooth things out. When we couldn't get any more sugar, Gene prowled over to a neighboring table to grab an unused bowl and the waiter confronted him, saying: "How much do you want? Five cubes? A half kilo? One kilo?" I couldn't help but laugh. This was getting ridiculous. As this food war was escalating, it probably was best that this was our last meal here.

Now I relished a good, thorough shower. Washing all the dirt of the streets of Delhi out, I felt great, renewed as I stepped into my freshly washed and pressed (by the floor boy) Western clothes. A wallet, a belt, pockets—this was really new and different. I was in my old Swabbies, spiffed up and ready to fly back into the Western world: London!

We gathered our four pieces of luggage (two rucksacks, a green suitcase full of souvenirs, and a sitar) and stepped into the waiting taxi. In twenty minutes we were at the overcrowded, hot, and sweaty Delhi International Airport. I was really tickled to be flying halfway home—tonight! I found the closest thing possible to a peaceful corner, killed a few roaches and other big bugs, and sat down to my journal. Then we checked into our Thai Airways flight, singing (that old song by The Rose Garden) "Next plane to London, leaving on runway #5." I watched the green bag and my tall, black sitar case disappear down the conveyor belt and I stepped up to be frisked. I asked the uniformed Sikh to squeeze my moneybelt again—it tickled. The bus shuttled us to the awaiting big DC-10-30 and we climbed into what seemed like a giant craft. I felt very confident and comfortable as I boarded. This is a good plane and a good airline.

Sept 5th   Delhi – LONDON   what a flight!

This was a huge plane, totally filled and it was festival seating so we found the last two seats together & readied ourselves for take off. It didn't really matter that we _____ because Gene sank into a quiet _____ _____ available on such a long _____ _____ be happy. My joints soo_ _____ _____ in the run- way, my _____ _____ _____ couldn't _____ but _____ _____ _____ _____ us leave India.

We stopped _____ _____ _____ never thought this trip would take me (back) and after 45 minutes we were back up in the dark sky. Thai airlines is great, gorgeous stewardesses make you want to go to Bangkok, corsages await everyone in their seat and everything from the take offs to the drinks goes smoothly.

I always think of the great fun I had flying Seattle, Amsterdam last year with Carl & Sue and with Ruth the _____ before and I wish I could have another little party. Airplanes can be such fun with the right company.

This was the first long through the night we had & I decided to break tradition and get some sleep even if it meant _____ _____ After in the flight movie, Annie Hall. I slept _____ _____ and it was 8:00 Indian time when I _____ _____ _____ _____ _____ _____

Tuesday, September 5: Delhi to London

What a flight! This was a huge plane, totally filled, and it was festival seating so we found the last two seats together and readied ourselves for take-off. My spirits soared with the plane as we sped down the runway, my head pressed back into the seat, and I couldn't help but smile with my eyes closed as I felt us leave India.

We stopped for fuel in Karachi (I never thought this trip would take me to Karachi) and after 45 minutes, we were back up in the dark sky. Thai Airways is great. Gorgeous stewardesses make you want to go to Bangkok, corsages await everyone in their seats, and everything from the take-offs to the drinks goes smoothly.

I always think of the great fun I had flying Seattle to Amsterdam last year with Carl and Sue, and with Ruth the year before. Airplane rides can be such fun. This was the longest, through-the-night flight I've had and I decided to break tradition and get some sleep, even if it meant missing Woody Allen in the in-flight movie, Annie Hall. I slept for a good four hours and it was 8:00 Indian time when I got up. After a stroll around the plane, people-watching, I asked a "stew" where we were and found out we were over Ankara. Wow, all the way to Turkey, so fast and easy! If I was on the ground now, I'd be on one of those miserable trans-Turkey, 24-hour bus rides. By the time I sat down again, we were passing Istanbul and then good old Svetoslav was down below me in Bulgaria. I bet he doesn't dream that I'm in Bulgarian airspace at this moment.

I marveled at the fifty days of adventure we'd lived since we said goodbye to Svetoslav in Plovdiv. And we just snoozed through that distance in four comfortable hours.

We were served a great breakfast: bacon and eggs! I had a great conversation with an Indian next to me, who was leaving his country and intending to take his doctoring trade ultimately to the USA. He had some interesting thoughts on India, world democracy, and medicine.

At 11:00 Indian time we landed in Frankfurt and, an hour later, we were flying again over the English Channel to London. It was strange to touch down where we had started and where we would end, but then fly on another hour only to return three days later. At 1:00 Indian time or (I think) 8:00 London time, we touched down smoothly at Heathrow Airport. Wow! London! This was halfway home. What a wonderful world it is. Outside it was about 55 degrees and the chaos was gone. Even in a crowded airport, things were orderly and even predictable. After India the term "it's all relative" is more pertinent than ever. We had done India, enjoyed it, and returned safely. I wasn't even sick. I was, needless to say, tickled to be in England—even for only two days.

London: cool and so civil...

I set my watch back five hours and it was 9 a.m., the beginning of a big day. Before we could enjoy all that London was ready to give us, we had business to take care of. We also made an abrupt adjustment in our budgeting mentality: Everything seemed terribly expensive after India. We decided to get the four-day unlimited subway and bus ticket for a staggering (by Indian standards) £8 or $16 each. Oh well, now we would be able to just hop on and off the otherwise expensive Tube without worrying about tickets. We picked up the encumbering sitar and green souvenir suitcase and took the Tube downtown to Victoria Station, where we checked the two big pieces. Now we only had very light rucksacks to carry around. We changed money (a lot, because I wanted a carefree, go-ahead-and-blow-it last couple of days of sightseeing) and we discovered a fantastic bargain train ticket to Frankfurt.

Transalpino, something new to me, offers nearly half-price train tickets to anywhere in Europe for us youngies under 26. That was the last big question of the trip: How expensive would a ticket back to Frankfurt be? That was answered very pleasantly: £20 or $40. Great! We got tickets for Thursday at 10:30 a.m. and would arrive in Frankfurt at midnight. We planned to just sack out at the station that last night before flying home in the morning. I couldn't have expected a smoother plan.

Just when we were getting our tickets, a royal commotion marched down the street. We ran out and London splashed all over us. In brilliant red and with

splendid precision, the Royal band welcomed us to London with plenty of British pomp. We found a picnic up in colorful Soho and sat down in a quaint park, so green and peaceful, with only the murmuring of the drunks and the distant Piccadilly traffic disturbing the overcast silence. As we made cheese sandwiches and guzzled our first cold, clean, unquestionably healthy milk in ages, an old vociferous drunk, who had long ago lost his last listener, still talked—to the benches, twigs, and birds. His voice was kind of like the music you hear but never listen to in an American grocery store. We enjoyed "our kind of food," so nice after iodine-tinted water and spicy rice all the time, and gave the drunk a double-cheese sandwich. He wanted a banana and our milk as well, but I shooed him away. He slobbered, "God bless ya, god bless ya" over and over as his voice got further and further away.

Now we split up, planning to meet at 6:45 at Liverpool Street Tube station. I wanted to wander around and take in a play and Gene wanted to do the things that a first-time visitor usually wants to do when he comes to London.

Soho is so nice. The Greenwich Village and Pigalle of London, you can just stroll down the streets, under the glittering invitations of strip joints and blinking sex supermarkets, telling old guys who need 10p that I'm just as broke, buying a tangerine from the friendliest man in the open-air market, passing old, sophisticated pubs propped up against 1970-ish movie theaters, boasting brightly of Saturday Night Fever. Tree-lined little parks that always seem to be in a mist, brick houses, white doors, and high polish brass knobs stand at attention and ladies chat just like yesterday, as they wait for the big, red double-decker that always comes. Time is wonderfully spent without plans in Soho.

One of my favorite pastimes in London is the theater. In my two days here I planned to see three, and one was a Tuesday matinee of a play called Sleuth. Gene said it was a good story and there weren't many Tuesday matinees to choose from so I took it in. It was a strange combination of detective thriller and comedy, not doing either exceptionally but doing both all right.

After the play I decided to dilly-dally for two hours on my way to meet Gene at Liverpool Street. Passing those collecting for a good cause, those painting terrible portraits for money (people would gather around and grimace as one guy mangled a poor Japanese girl on canvas), and barking salesmen trying to make dull newspapers exciting, I came to Trafalgar Square, where people feed pigeons, climb on stone lions, and take pictures of people on lions and pigeons on people.

I was in the mood to sit and enjoy. London was characteristically overcast, and the cool was delightful after India. I sat at the edge of a fountain, looking up at Lord Nelson and down at hordes of pigeons. I laughed at a cute little guy who offered the pigeons the world and they wouldn't even nibble a seed. He looked so funny and frustrated. He shared his seeds with me and together we won the patronage of a little flock. Soon we had pigeons all over us and no more seeds. Then there's always the mean little three-year-old who is determined to step on a pigeon. A vagrant told me that if you manage to grab one and slam it onto the pavement, its head pops off.

After a stroll down The Strand, I met Gene as planned. I called the Szpers (family friends who are usually happy to put me up when I'm in town) and they said they were entertaining and couldn't put us up but we could drop by for some tea. Tea was nice and I wanted to see them, but now we faced a night out in the cold. We called a few hostels and all were full, so we decided to head out to Ilford (they lived nearly at the end of the Tube system) for tea and worry about our bed later. I hoped Mrs. Szper would let us even sleep on the floor, but I definitely didn't want to put them on the spot. They are a dear old troll-like Polish couple—both hunched over and always smiling—and I would rather sit in a Tube station all night than take advantage of them. I figured the problem was that she was reluctant to give us anything other than first-class hospitality, when we would be tickled to have a 6' x 2' piece of dry carpet to sleep on.

Mr. Szper opened the door and couldn't get over my shaggy appearance. I showed them my passport photo to prove it was good old me and we sat down for dinner, with lovely cold beer, tea, and cake. They were both doing really well. I hadn't seen them for three years but we are amazingly comfortable in our friendship. They didn't get my card yet from Varanasi, warning of our arrival in London, so this was quite unexpected to them.

We goofed around for a while and, since their guests were up in Scotland and we assured them that we would love to sleep in their sheets, we were invited to spend the night. After a long but fascinating trip through Mr. Szper's crazy youth, and a close look at all the scientific stuff he's had published, I couldn't disguise my state of tiredness any longer and we excused ourselves to a wonderful British bed. To need a blanket and have one is happiness.

Wednesday, September 6: London

I woke up at 7 a.m., anxious to get downtown, mostly for Gene's sake. He had lots of work to do for the last half of his two-day, whirlwind London tour. We were served a nice traditional breakfast (just like past trips) by Mr. Szper. From my experience, England knows only one two-course breakfast: fruit juice and Corn Flakes, followed by cold, crispy toast, eggs, and fried sausage. I always feel rude to be so preoccupied by London when I'm at the Szper's. But they explored the world in their youth and they understood. We talked for a while but still got an early start, making it downtown shortly after 9 a.m.

After India, London came with culture shock in reverse.

Once again, we split up for the day, planning to meet at Piccadilly Circus at 6:00 p.m. When time is very limited, it's most efficiently spent independently. Gene headed for the Tower of London, soaked in bloody history, and I went to the British Museum to appreciate it with much more background than the last time I was there.

The British Museum, like few others in the world, really frustrates the visitor with wide interests and limited time. I have learned so much about art, culture, and the world since I was last there in 1975 that I needed to go through the whole bloody museum again. I only had a couple of hours so I limited myself to ancient art. After my ancient art class at the UW and my trip to Egypt, I really had lots that I wanted to see. I concentrated on Assyria and Mesopotamian cultures, whipping quickly through Egypt, and skipping Greece and Rome altogether. Then I dashed over to catch the 11 a.m. lecture on the Magna Carta at the Magna Carta. I learned a lot in that 30-minute talk, standing right over the documents that symbolized the rise of the common people over kings. After one last look at the Lions Gate of Khorsabad and some sculpture from Nineveh, I moved along.

After eggs, beans, and chips for 60p at my favorite little Soho greasy spoon, I paid £1.50 and really enjoyed the new tourist attraction in Piccadilly called The London Experience. That's a good name. With seven screens before me, I was taken through 2,000 action-packed years of London in one hour. There's something about British nationalism that really moves me. I think I love this country more than any other outside of my own, and I'm almost brought to tears when I am overcome by England's pride and spirit. The Queen, the Blitz, the pubs, the bobbies, the buses, and the warm people shining through those fantastic accents. Battling civilly and doggedly for greatness and continued splendor, she isn't what she used to be in some ways, but she'll always be the same in other ways. There's really nothing like Great Britain.

Now I had an hour to stroll before finding the Drury Lane Theatre and taking in A Chorus Line. I was excited to see this famous and very popular New York show. I got one of the cheapest seats for £2 but ended up with a great spot on the ground floor, one row behind the £4 seats, since they don't use the balcony for matinee performances. Much better than yesterday's play, I was all wrapped up in the orchestra and cast of 20 or 30. A Chorus Line is indeed first-class entertainment.

With another piece of free time, I slowly made my way back up to Piccadilly Circus and there sat Gene, reading a lousy London newspaper, sitting in the middle of all the wasted, bleary-eyed heads, freaks, weirdos, and tourists who sit for hours on Piccadilly Circus, watching the one-ring circus where Soho and stylish-theater-London converge ungracefully on this sooty center of all kinds of London life, but especially nightlife. We shared our day's experiences, refusing sales pitches for acid and hash, and then decided to head out for dinner.

Mr. Szper recommended Ye Old Cheshire Cheese, a pub with "the best steak-and-kidney pie in London." We found it very crowded on Fleet Street. It looked great until we noticed the £3.50 minimum charge. We didn't have £7 for dinner so we walked around, checking out other pubs and sampling a few drinks. I had a shandy, which is beer and lemonade, and later I tried a very strong beer called Barley wine. We had a hard time finding a pub serving food but, on our way down the King's Road in Chelsea, we got our shepherd's pie and steak-and-kidney pie. It's quite a shock not to be able to afford restaurant food after enjoying the power of our relative wealth in India.

We went to the King's Road Theatre to see *The Rocky Horror Picture Show*. It's been a hit musical for six years and, after seeing the movie at least eight or ten times back in Seattle, I was finally going to get the chance to see it live on stage—the play that the movie is based on. It was quite different than the movie, not as outrageous, but very entertaining. We had no trouble staying awake during the musical, but the long ride home was dreadful. We walked, bused, and subway-ed for well over an hour. I was so tired, I barely made the trip. We got back to the Szpers' at about midnight and they were still up. We talked for a while, but only a short while, and in a few minutes, I was fast asleep.

Thursday, September 7: London to Frankfurt

Now the trip was as good as over and I was happy. All we had to do was travel to Frankfurt and catch our plane home. Mr. Szper burned us some toast to have with a salty omelet and bid us a warm farewell. He said, as we walked out the door, "Come again!" so I think he enjoyed our company and extended my welcome. He and his wife are so nice. It's neat to see two people so right for each other. After 50 years, still kissing each other goodbye in the morning and looking good to each other, with memories and love blotting out fatness and wrinkles. They have grown old gracefully, but it must be very hard for a crazy-active guy like Mr. Szper to be retired and sitting at home all day while his wife is still working.

We waved goodbye and hurried downtown to Victoria Station. I get nervous when there's very little extra time for a crucial connection like this one. We quickly picked up our checked luggage and made a few rounds of the station trying to sell our half-used, four-day Tube passes. I found a British girl who was happy to give me a pound for a pass and we traded. Immediately, a plain-clothed copper introduced himself and flashed his badge.

"Didn't you just give this girl a pass and take from her a pound?"

"Why yes, officer, I did."

"You could be charged criminally and brought to court."

"Oh my, I didn't realize I couldn't sell this! I have a train to catch in ten minutes!"

A second bobby appeared and they both acted like they had caught Al Capone. Terrible thoughts raced through my mind. If I missed this train, I didn't know how I would catch the plane in Frankfurt. Then, as they figured I had been shaken up enough, they said sternly, "Okay, give us the passes and give her back her pound." Whew! We walked off quickly and got safely on the train before anything else could happen.

At 10:35 a.m. we rolled out of London, and by noon we were in gray, drizzly Dover. The customs process was amazingly smooth and fast, quite a contrast to Asian customs. Soon we were sailing across the peaceful English Channel with terrible visibility. (Every time I hop a ship to cross this 30-mile-long pass, I wonder why France and Britain can't find a way to build the tunnel they've been squabbling about constructing for years now.) We relaxed for the four-hour cruise, having a picnic and not spending any money. We didn't want to spend a penny more on this trip. By dinner time, we were cruising through Belgium and enjoying a good conversation with a British girl who had just started her trip. Later, I found an empty compartment and goofed around with my sitar. At one point, a formally dressed Belgian businessman joined our compartment.

He piled his suitcase on top of my rucksack. I jumped up and said, "Tomatoes," motioning to my rucksack. He replied, "Pizza."

We rolled down the Rhine, past the floodlit castles I had seen back on July 13 when I headed to Frankfurt to meet Gene. The big circle had been made. It was midnight and we wasted no time catching the train out to the airport. We decided not to worry about changing money in order to buy the 1.50 DM (75 cents) ticket for the 11-minute ride. We both just hoped that the conductor wouldn't get to us so fast. We chose the middle of the train, figuring that would be the last part to be checked for tickets. There we sat, sweating out the minutes. Ten minutes to go, nine, eight…Then, wouldn't you know it, the gruff-looking conductor appeared. It was obvious that this guy would put up with no funny business. We explained that we had just arrived from London and hoped to buy the ticket from him. He spoke only enough English to chew us out and he lit into us with relish. He threatened to carry out the 40 DM ($20) penalty. We looked at him in disbelief, repeating that we were just going to the Lufthavn. Finally, he took $3 from us for the tickets, and we stepped off at the airport, kind of chuckling. We had tried the exact same trick five years ago on the last day of our high school graduation whirlwind Europe trip and had just made it to the airport before the conductor came.

Now it was close to 1:00 a.m. and we found a wonderful warm, quiet, and comfy sofa to sack out on. This airport is the ideal place to crash and sleep for free. I locked all my luggage to the couch, careful to loop in my sitar, and slept.

Friday, September 8: Frankfurt to Seattle… Home!

I slept very nicely, considering my bedroom, and at 7 a.m. the airport was busy, and I was too. We had breakfast, realizing that we had bought too much food in London, and then I changed into my new Indian-style clothes. It felt good to be back in my loose, baggy, breezy, comfortable "Indian whites." We goofed around on the sitar and I'm so glad I got it. I believe it's growing on me. Then we packed up our bags for the flight and checked in for our Pacific Western flight. We had some time and some film to blow so we went outside for some photo fun. I got some great shots of the "Overland to India" map. We got a guy to take a shot of us "truckin'" just like we did five years ago at the end of our trip, at the same spot.

By 11:00 a.m. we had gone through the tight security check and were sitting just behind the wing on our Boeing 707. How nice to be flying home. The stewardesses were great, everything was fine, and again I smiled with my head pressed back against my seat as we ripped down the runway. Taking off is ecstasy—the Gs make it even more so, as if physically impressing on me what a blessing this experience has been. It's so clean and easy. In a few minutes I looked down and saw Amsterdam, and then we left Europe behind, Britain behind, and open seas ahead.

Charters are great for free drinks and I really felt like some rum. I had a rum and orange juice, and also drank Gene's rum and Coke. I had two more drinks and, with the way those stews mixed 'em, I was sprawled all over the wing. Stupidly, I overdid it and threw up over Iceland. Really out of it, I went through two barf bags and slept across Greenland and totally missed Hudson's Bay. If nothing else, that was a good way to get some sleep. I felt better by the Northwest Territories, and we were served a great dinner of steak, twice-baked potatoes, and apple pie. Gene and I both agreed that apple pie and cheese are strange partners. The flight was passing quickly and, before I knew it, Vancouver was just below us, Mt. Baker cheered me on just outside my window, and coming into view was my hometown—with its neighborly hills, proud Space Needle, and evergreen spirit. Moments later, Gene was in the arms of his parents, and I was wrapped in a bundle of family love. So thankful to have gone away. So thankful to have lived the Hippie Trail. And so happy to now be home.

Afterword (2022)

People say you can't do this trip today. I disagree. This trip was not Iran, Afghanistan, and India. It was a 23-year-old, on the verge of adulthood, getting to know the world. That same world and those same 23-year-olds are still out there, waiting to connect. In my work, I hear from these young globe-trotters all the time: travelers—both young men and young women—who are venturing beyond the world of "tourism" to become friends with the world. And I'm inspired by their stories.

With today's modernity, technology, and globalization seeming to permeate and homogenize our world, it's easy to think there simply are no more Hippie Trails. But I believe anyone can still stow away on the reality express, as I did back in 1978. They can get their fingers dirty in other cultures, wallop their ethnocentrism, and come home with that most valuable souvenir: a broader perspective.

This has been the story of the trip that laid the foundation for me to be more than a travel writer—to be an evangelist for the notion that good travel is more than selfies and bucket lists. Travelers learn that fear is for people who don't get out much; that culture shock is a good thing, the growing pains of a broader perspective; and that we're all children of God—and by traveling, we get to know the family. This journal was written before any of those catchphrases I now use so routinely in my lectures and writing existed. And this trip primed me for the career that followed—guidebooks, bus tours, TV shows…*Europe Through the Back Door, Mona Winks, Travel as a Political Act.*

I believe that if more people could have such a transformative experience—especially in their youth—it could help make our world a more just and stable place. We'd recognize that the challenges that will confront our society going forward will be blind to borders. Hopefully, those challenges will be tackled by people working together…the family of nations working hand-in-hand. And most fundamentally, travelers learn that the world is a good place. It's filled with joy and with love and with good people. And—young or old, rich or poor, backpack or rolling suitcase—the best way to understand that is to experience it firsthand. To get out there and get to know our neighbors. To build not walls, but bridges.

Thanks for joining me on my "trip of a lifetime." And best wishes on yours.

Saturday   Aug. 19th.   Tansen - Pokara

Our hotel didn't wake us but the roosters did.
At 4:45 we were up. I surveyed my body - no bugs
or Nepali leeches were found! We ordered eight
little Nepali eggs boiled and said we'd be back in
ten minutes after a quick run through the town to see
what we saw last night by lantern light today by
sun light. Most of the town was awake & heading for
the Buddhist Temple. We peeked in. The same old
music was droning away. The express bus was leaving
for Pokara in a few minutes so & we crammed
down our eggs, saving buscuits, pills + tang for the bus,
and, after a picture of our hotel's sign saying, "For
homely. Please get here".

Running, we just hopped into the early bus. It was
6:00 and it was pulling out. This was a local bus
but quite alright. Plenty of room, only very fast stops
and costing about $1.25 each for the 6 hour, 120 kilometer
ride. The bus went 12 miles or 20 km every hour and
we pulled into Pokara at exactly noon.

From Tansen we wound through the lush mountains
braving rock slides + nearly washed out roads. At one
point one guy got out and ran down the one lane
"highway" tossing fallen stones out of the way. As our
rusty old bus clung to the tenuous edge I hung my head
out the window looking straight down at a vigorous
river, long + lonely rope foot bridges, thatched huts and
green dripping terraces. My spirit soared as we climbed
deeper into the ancient kingdom of Nepal. We passed
through several small town + villages. Most were no more
than a row of huts along the roadside. Until recently,
Pokara, Nepal's second largest town, was accessible only
by air or trail. This road + the one to Katmandu,
200 km to The East, really opened up this region. Western
tee-shirts + Eveready batteries had found their way in
but I don't think alot has changed here. The villagers
still squat wide-eyed as the busses pass through. I didn't
see a single other westerner from the border to Pokara.

The kilometers passed slowly as we neared Pokara and
blue sky began beating the clouds away. As we
entered the beautiful Pokara Valley the bus became
very crowded. For the last long thirty minutes
I had a powerful Nepali woman nearly shoving
me out the window.

Transportation statistics-

Frankfurt - Beograd - 23 hrs train $80
Beograd - Sofia 10 hrs train $16
Sofia - Istanbul 15 hrs train $16
Istanbul - Tehran 63 hrs bus $32
   actual time w/ accident - 4 nights
   + 3 days.
Tehran - Mashed 18 hrs bus $6
Mashad - Border of Afganistan 3 hrs bus $2
   Iran-Afgan border 5 hours
Border - Herat 3½ hours bus $1.50
Herat - Kabul 14 hour bus $5
   Qadafi bus co. = great
Kabul - Peshawar 8 hours bus $2.50
   Pakistan Bus Co. - good
   includes 3 hours at border
Peshawar - Lahore 12 hours train $3.50
   1st class $3.50 2nd class $2
   we broke trip to sleep in Rawalpindi
Lahore - Amritsar 4 hours bus or taxi $1
   including 2 hours at the border

Total Frankfurt - India (Amritsar) $165
   about 180 hours including
   border + other hassles

Amritsar - Jammu 7 hours train $1 2nd class
                                     $5 1st class sleeper
Jammu - Srinagar 12 hours bus $2.50
Srinagar - Delhi 1 hour plane $30
Delhi - Gorakhpur 1 hour plane ??
Tansen - Pokara 6 hours bus $1.50
Pokara - Katmandu ½ hour plane $10
Katmandu - Patna 1 hour plane $20
Patna - Varanasi 5 hours train 1.50 2nd class
Varanasi - Agra 13 hours train 4.00 2nd cl. sleeper
Agra - Jaipur 8 hours train 2.00 2nd cl sleeper
Jaipur - Delhi 6 hours bus + truck $1.50
Delhi - London 12 hours plane $340 Thai budget fare.
London - Frankft 13 hours train $40 yo

Accomodations—

Price for double (w/o food)

Date	Place	Description	Price for double (w/o food)
July 14	Train	Munich – Yugoslavia	—
15	Beograd	sleep in train station	—
16, 17	Plovdiv	svati's	—
18	Train	Plovdiv – Istanbul	$7
19	Istanbul	Hotel Agan 175 lira	
	Istanbul – Erzurum		
20	Bus		$1.40
21	Middle of Turkey, 5 hours in lousy hotel, 30 lira		
22	Erzurum	lousy hotel 35 lira	$2.80
23	Bus	long night	
24	Teheran	Tourist Hotel Amir Kabir A hole!	6.00
25, 26	Tehran	Abe's place – great guy.	
27, 28	Mashad	campground, great swimming pool	3.00
29, 30, 31	Herat	Mowafaq Hotel – 1st class	$5.00
		great food, pool, friendly, clean central location 200 afs	$3.80
August 1, 2, 3	Kabul	Sina Hotel – next to Mustafa hotel near chicken street. Quiet friendly, nice courtyard w b-fast	
4	Rawalpindi	A no name flop house	$1.00
5	Lahore	Hotel Menora – 41 Mcleod Rd Phone- 56188 great, friendly, with private shower WC + fan across from Hotel Lahore, central	6.50
6	Train	Amritsar – Jammu	
7, 8, 9, 13	Srinagar	Muzaffer Houseboat 80 rs ($10) for double, full board + complete service.	4.00
10	Gulmarg	Kingsley Hotel – very nice	2.50
11, 12	Lake Nagin	"The Ritz" houseboat, Truely delux $6 each for 3 meals, great servants + peace	5.00
14, 15, 16, 17	Delhi	YMCA Jai Singh St. 43 rs 6x6 each	8.00
18	Tansen	Siddhartha Hotel - the nicest available	1.50
19, 20, 21	Pokara	Hotel Mount Annapurna, the best place so far – totally first class with great restaurant.	11.00
22, 23, 24, 25	Katmandu	Sugat Hotel, Basantapur Square	4.00
26, 27	Varanasi	Hotel International, big clean + air conditioned. Not great but OK	8.00
28	Train	Varanasi – Agra	—
29	Agra	Grand Hotel 75 rs for A/c B+B Air Cond. good cheap restaurant, great service, room, bath + location	7.00
30	Train + Jaipur	IInd class sleeper + Tourist Bungalo	2.00
31	Jaipur	Khetri House, B + B 77rs Fantastic stately living Maharashas palace	6.50
Sept 1, 2, 3	Delhi	YMCA Jai Singh St.	8.00
4	Plane	Flying over Asia	—
5, 6	London	The Szpet's house	—

With each journal, I kept an appendix filled with the nitty gritty data on practical details: transportation times and costs, hotel listing with cost. While I didn't know how yet, I had a feeling such details might be helpful to other travelers. Of course, within a few years, collecting details like these became a big part of my work.

only rarely and the scenery was 'dramatic'.
we passed through a high rugged mountain
pass right next the the highest mountain
in western Asia.

The Spaniards played the Rolling Stones on
their tape recorder, we read, enjoyed the
scenery and I made friends with a
gorgeous little Persian girl in front of
me. I took some pictures of her that may
be prize winners.

After 12:00 we came out of the
and into a hot humid sticky plain
just went on + on. The plywood
towns all looked the same + so
to slow down traffic. The

before going back down we decided to enjoy the
r of kathmandu and eat a box of Glucose bis
pened the little box, took out a biscuit & like by
rude but effective monkey swiped it right out of
d! I was startled. He wanted more & frightened
ly tossed him another. I quickly ate one of he
me at me demanding more. I stood up + beg
flee but he prowled right after me. A friend
ed him & I was about to be viciously double
amed. Nervously and not wanting to be ripped to
bons by a holy monkey I tossed him the entire box and
jumped atop a small temple &, very humanly, ate the
uits one by one. I was totally defeated + even sli
uled, which I will have to treat with iodine
y be holy but they're far from clean.
we walked back down and returned to Durbar S

Explore Europe
Browse thousands of articles, videos, and money-saving travel tips to help plan your dream trip.

Travel Forum
Learn, ask, share—our online community of savvy travelers is a great resource for trip planning.

TV Shows
Watch *Rick's Steves' Europe* TV episodes—for free and on demand.

Radio Interviews
Listen to Rick's radio show as he explores the world with his guests.

Rick's App
Download Audio Europe™ to get free self-guided walking tours of Europe's top sights.

Travel Newsletter
Subscribe to Rick's free monthly email packed with European travel information.

Rick Steves Tours
Experience Europe the "Rick Steves way" on a small group bus tour.

Classroom Europe®
Our free resource with 500+ short video clips from the TV show.

Read more about Rick's travel experiences in *For the Love of Europe*

An inspiring collection of 100 of Rick's most unforgettable memories, gathered from over four decades of European travel. Savor the travel thrills from Portugal to the Peloponnese and discover your own favorite slice of Europe.

© 2022 Rick Steves' Europe, Inc.
130 4th Ave N, Edmonds, WA 98020

Edited by Rosie Leutzinger,
Amy Duncan, and Lisa Werner

Art direction by Rhonda Pelikan

Design and layout by Heather Locke

Photography by Rick Steves and
Gene Openshaw (unless otherwise noted)